Isaac Lindo Mocatta

The Jewish Armoury

Isaac Lindo Mocatta

The Jewish Armoury

ISBN/EAN: 9783743311299

Manufactured in Europe, USA, Canada, Australia, Japa

Cover: Foto ©ninafisch / pixelio.de

Manufactured and distributed by brebook publishing software (www.brebook.com)

Isaac Lindo Mocatta

The Jewish Armoury

INDEX.

	PAGE.
PREFACE.	v.

CHAP. I.—Four important words in connection with Judaism—ONE—EVERLASTING—TRUE—PERFECT ... 1— 23

II.—The Divine laws and ordinances inculcated in the Mosaic dispensation, which are *preeminently distinguished* for their sublime morality and practical utility ... 24— 56

III.—A review of sundry Mosaic laws and ordinances, such as need close investigation to enable the cursory reader of the Sacred Volume to arrive at a full conviction of their supreme excellence ... 57— 85

IV.—On the Immortality of the Soul as an article of Jewish belief, practically and inferentially demonstrated in the Pentateuch, and repeatedly referred to in other portions of the Sacred Volume ... 86— 98

V.—Short biographical sketches from Sacred and Profane History, proving to demonstration the efficacy of the Mosaic code of laws upon individual character ... 99—135

VI.—Extracts from the writings of some of the most enlightened men in Christendom showing that the Jewish belief in the Unity of God coincides with their own convictions; that in the main they admit the Mosaic code to be alike practical and useful; that they highly appreciate many traits peculiar to the Hebrew race; finally, extracts from works written by Jewish authors on their own national characteristics and social position.. 136—179

PREFACE.

The Jewish Association for the diffusion of Religious Knowledge thus concludes one of its latest Reports,—"The many influences which are at work in this present age of materalism, when all religions are being subject to the severest tests and trials, render it necessary that we should endeavour to place in the hands of the followers of our Holy Faith—the first as well as foundation of all revealed religion—weapons with which to combat the attacks from without, and even from within. This can only be effected by the dissemination amongst our co-religionists of a clear and correct knowledge of Judaism and its observances."

With the above quotation vividly impressed on his mind, the writer takes up his pen earnest in the furtherance of a like object, and, as he does so with extreme diffidence he trusts that no presumption will be imputed to him, either in regard to the title he has chosen, or to the assurance he has displayed in following in the wake of an association, which has already achieved so much, and justly gained the attention and high consideration of the entire Jewish community.

Before proceeding to offer a few remarks regarding the main purport of these pages, the author would be permitted to make some slight reference to his last religious work, viz., "MORAL BIBLICAL GLEANINGS," indeed, both books have this common object, to concentrate and bring into relief all that is most valuable and instructive in the Holy volume. In the "Gleanings" are to be found, under especial headings, a variety of practical precepts with a short biography of numerous Israelites of old, who, considering those precepts their best heirloom, strove sedulously to practice and follow them out, and having succeeded therein, left us a legacy of imperishable names, names which adorn the annals of History, and will ever be admired and revered by all of every sect or creed, who can appreciate true merit and agree to stamp the character of man according to its moral excellence.

In the present little volume the author has for object to bring before his co-religionists an epitome of the very many facts and arguments which have tended to give strength and permanency to the Jewish faith, besides other data, avoiding all that is discursive; and by thus bringing them together in the most compact form possible, he trusts good service will be rendered to the cause of religion, and that these pages will meet the wishes of those persons who, lacking either time or inclination to peruse long controversial works, are, nevertheless, desirous of having placed before them a fair exposition of Judaism and its Laws, whilst it will enable the enlightened Christian to cast a thoughtful and appreciative glance over a summary of those numerous beautiful ordinances and holy truths which have given, and will assuredly continue to give, life, stability, and lasting vitality to the religion of the Israelite.

Preface.

As a book entitled "The Jewish Armoury" may be deemed incomplete by some readers without it contains especial reference to the views expounded by David and the teachings of the Prophets, it will be well to state here that the writer had proposed concluding this volume with two chapters devoted thereto, and it is solely on account of enfeebled health that he foregoes his original intention. The enforced curtailment of this work would have proved a source of greater regret to its author had he not been impressed with the belief that any additional strength imparted to Judaism through the Psalms and the Books of the Prophets is mostly, if not solely, due to the fact that their writers, true to the ancestral faith, undeviatingly upheld the Mosaic code and demonstrated in the most impassioned language how greatly they appreciated each precept, each ordinance contained therein. The teachings of these chosen servants of God are simply supplementary, and though of inestimable value in themselves, cannot dwarf in the slightest degree the mighty structure of Mosaism.

But could it by possibility be conceded that *some few verses* both in the Psalms and in the Prophets militated against the doctrines and laws set forth by the great Law giver, yet on how slender a thread do they hang when weighed with the mass of evidence that can be brought forth against any such construction, and even these selected verses utterly lose their assumed significance in the minds of the unprejudiced when they reflect on the fact that these props to another creed have, in nearly every instance, been wrested from their true meaning, their true intent, through a strange perversion and an undoubted mistranslation from the original language. Nevertheless, as Judaism has been assailed at various epochs through the mistaken or ill-directed zeal of many a novice in Hebrew literature, it is fortunate that there are some valuable Jewish works on the subject of these controversial verses, and the author believes that it will be opportune here to draw the attention of his readers to three books of sterling merit, wherein are to be found the most undeniable proofs that these isolated and mistranslated verses, so well calculated to mislead, are easily refuted and altogether fail to weaken or undermine a religion which has survived repeated attacks during long centuries. The names of these valuable works are, 1stly, "FAITH STRENGTHENED," translated from the Hebrew by the revered Mr. Moses Mocatta; 2ndly, "A COURSE OF SERMONS" by Dr. Hermann Adler, 3rdly, "THE DEICIDES" by J. Cohen, translated from the French by Miss Anna Maria Goldsmid.

In conclusion, the author, while expressing the hope that some allowance will be made for any shortcomings in this work, is yet sanguine enough to believe that it will in a measure subserve the object, the intent which first gave it birth and then quickened it into existence.

BRIGHTON,
    NOVEMBER, 1877.

THE JEWISH ARMOURY.

Chapter I.

There are four words of superlative importance when taken in connection with the Jewish religion, and indeed it would be impossible to overrate their rare significance to the Jew, since on them is based the whole structure of his sublime and venerable faith; we allude to the words, ONE, EVERLASTING, TRUE, PERFECT.

Now, it might well be supposed, that no amount of ingenuity could pervert these simple, yet all comprehensive words from their obvious meanings, but since they are, nevertheless, often distorted or wrenched from their original signification, it may be well to direct our attention to these symbols of the Israelitish creed, and endeavour to show that the Jews cannot by any possibility interpret them otherwise than have their forefathers throughout past centuries; but, holding them to be the most unequivocal words to be found in the Holy volume, they will assuredly continue to make them a standpoint, so long as language is capable of conveying definite, accurate, and distinct ideas to the human mind.

Referring, firstly, to the UNITY of God, represented by the word "One," which is again and again repeated throughout the Scriptures in reference to the Deity,—it would seem incredible that any question could possibly be raised as to the precise sense intended to be conveyed through it, and the more so, because frequently found in conjunction with the most distinct, the most emphatic negation of Divine plurality; nevertheless, the absolute Unity of God,—the fundamental, the vital principle of Judaism, and treasured as such by all Israelites throughout their long chequered history,—is most certainly not regarded under the same point of view by those who believe in the Trinity. It may, therefore, be well to cull some all important verses from the Sacred volume, and show the grounds whereon the Jew holds so tenaciously to this conviction, as also the authority whereon he bases his implicit, his undying belief.

The first commandment of that Decalogue, which was delivered direct from Heaven to the Jewish nation, and has ever been held in high reverence by those of a different creed, opens with the personal pronoun of the *singular* number, "I," which in no one instance, when applied to mortals, has served to convey the idea of plurality. This monosyllable, then, being universally symbolic of unity, of oneness, cannot in fairness be wrested from its general signification when applied to the Deity, particularly since it is often coupled with some such negation to plurality as gives it even additional force; for example, "I, the Lord of Hosts, am the first and the last, *and besides me there is no God.*" And again we find this solemn declaration: Hosea 13, v. iv, "I am the Lord thy God, thou shalt know no God but me, *for there is no Saviour besides me*"; also, "I am God, *there is no other, and my glory will I not give to another*,"—a sentence which of itself bears the imprint of Omniscience, a foreknowledge of what was to occur long centuries after, as indeed does also the following verse, Is. ch. 43, v. xi., "*I*, even I am the Lord, and *beside ME there is no Saviour*": in which quotation it is notable that the singular number is *twice* repeated, as also when the Lord proclaimed, Deut. ch. 32, v. xxxix, "I am *He*, and there is no God with *me*," or again, Is. ch. 43, v. xxv., "I, even I, am *He* who blotteth out thy transgressions." It is further deserving of notice that to the letter "I" is frequently affixed the all important, because unequivocal monosyllable "One," as for example, Is. ch. 60, v. xvi, "I, the Lord, am thy Saviour, thy Redeemer, the mighty *One* of Israel." Also the forcible words "only" and "alone," adding thereby fresh significance, and, it might be thought, precluding the possibility of attaching to it a plural meaning; indeed, had we solely the heaven-sent article of belief, "I, the Lord thy God am *One* God," it would surely suffice to fix this truth indelibly in the heart. Then again, the proof of this first personal pronoun being intended to represent unity in the Godhead may be found in the fact of its being so frequently coupled with words of deepest import, viz., "the Eternal," "the King," "Jehovah," the latter especially being a name which certainly conveys a distinct idea of individuality to the human mind, and when regarded as the Hebrew equivalent to the sacred appellation, "I AM," carries with it a hallowed sense of that Divine essence which knows no subdivision, no plurality. It may here also be observed that the singular pronoun, "Thou," is always used in the Pentateuch, the Psalms, and the Prophets, when reference is made to the Deity; as for example, "Thou, the Holy One of Israel," "Thou, the Most High, will judge his people."

It may, however, be advanced that the pronoun "We" is occasionally employed in the Old Testament when referring to the Supreme, yet surely no proof of plurality is hereby afforded, since this monosyllable is used in most languages in lieu of the singular form when the object is to intensify authority, or give force of utterance, as in the case of a Monarch on issuing a decree, or an author when seeking to be especially impressive. Nor may we overlook the use of the word "Elohim," which, having a plural termination, might be open to misconception, were it not frequently employed also in reference to a messenger of God, or to some human authority, as, for instance, we find Manoch exclaiming after he had perceived "an angel of the Lord," "we shall surely die, for we 'have seen Elohim.'" And still more to the point are the words of God Himself to Moses; Ex. ch. 7, v. i., "Behold, I have made thee *an Elohim* to Pharaoh," which, of itself, might amply suffice to prove that the expression "Elohim," like the pronoun "We," is used to signify authority in the *individual*, since here it is indubitable that Moses alone is alluded to. Furthermore, the pure spirituality of the Deity is clearly inculcated by the Lawgiver when addressing the multitudes who had been eye witnesses of the delivery of the Law at Mount Sinai, he says: Deut. ch. 4, v. xv., "Take ye therefore good heed unto yourselves; for ye saw no manner of similitude on the day that the Lord spake unto you in Horeb out of the midst of the fire: lest ye corrupt yourselves and make you a graven image, the similitude of any figure, the likeness of male or female."

Once let us permit ourselves to conceive either plurality or materialism in the Supreme, and we have but too surely dwarf in our minds the Great Lord of all, which fact doubtless caused Moses, not only to prohibit the people under various penalties from setting up graven images, but also led him to proclaim again and again the incorporeality and invisibility of the God of Israel.

The glorious truth of the Unity of the Deity has for long centuries been cherished and upheld by the Hebrew as the fundamental principle, the very keystone of his faith; the words in Deut. ch. 6, *v.* iv.: "Hear, O Israel, the Lord our God, the Lord is ONE," first lisped in earliest childhood, never cease to form the daily prayer of each devout Jew till that final hour arrives, when, in heartfelt and pious accents, he seals this life-long conviction, by their utterance with his latest breath. Truly this grand and solemn article of belief, the heaven-given heirloom of the knowledge of the Unity of the Godhead, can never be lost to the House of Israel or remain indefinitely obscured to the world so long as the Jew is true to himself, to his children, and to his God.*

Proceeding next to consider the word "Everlasting" in connection with the Mosaic dispensation, which, although a word of itself, amply

---

* At chap. 5 will be found the views of many enlightened Christians on this all important doctrine, coinciding most remarkably with this primary article of the Jewish faith. Surely it is to the belief of the oneness and pure spirituality of the Deity that we must ascribe the following sublime idea of the great Unitarian philosopher, Sir Isaac Newton: "His centre is everywhere, His circumference nowhere."

demonstrates that the Law given by God through Moses was to endure to all times, we yet find that though frequently repeated in various portions of Scripture, it is further supplemented by many hardly less positive affirmations of permanent duration in such expressions as these, "always," "for ever and ever," "from everlasting to everlasting," "to all generations." For example, we find in Is. ch. 24, v. v., "The earth is defiled under the inhabitants thereof; because they have transgressed the laws, changed the ordinance, broken the *everlasting covenant:*" again, Is. ch. 40, v. viii., "The grass withereth, the flower fadeth, but the word of God shall stand for ever;" also in Deut. ch. 7, v. ix., "Know that the Lord, the faithful God, who keepeth covenant and mercy with them that love him and *keep his commandments to a thousand generations;*" again Deut. ch. 11, v. i., "Thou shalt love the Lord thy God and keep his statutes, his judgments, and his commandments *always.*" And in Numbers ch. 15, v. xv., "One ordinance shall be both for you and for the stranger that sojourneth with you, an ordinance *for ever* in your generations." But possibly there is no quotation

that could be selected from the Holy Volume which would better serve to prove the intended durability of the Law than the following :—
Is. ch. 24, v. iv., "*My covenant will I not break, nor alter the thing that has gone out of my lips, saith the Lord.*" Surely here we have the clearest evidence that the Mosaic code is to be both permanent and immutable; indeed, to admit the bare possibility that any occurrence could happen which might lead to a modification of what God Himself has once decreed, and this, in the most emphatic, most unqualified language, is little short of impugning the Divine attributes of Omnipotence and Omniscience. Truly, that charter of Sinai upon which the Eternal set His signet, and which has stood the test of centuries, will, to quote the words of David, Ps. ch. 105, v. viii., "Endure to one thousand generations." That this was the conviction of those faithful servants of God, who were permitted to read the future and prophesy in the name of the Most High, admits of no shadow of doubt, else, instead of explicitly holding out the assurance of the perpetuity of the Law, and devising every possible means of disseminating the Holy Ordinances among the people,

exhorting their observance alike by threats and entreaties, and sparing no labour which could contribute thereto, these inspired prophets would assuredly have made known any forthcoming change and prepared their disciples for it. Without this firm conviction would Ezra and Nehemiah have written out the law and enforced its fulfilment? Would the positive command for the observance of the Sabbath, and various other inculcations have been again and again insisted on by each succeeding prophet of the Lord from the time of Isaiah to that of Malachi? Indeed, the last words of the latter at the very close of Bible history, ch. 4, v. iv., "*Remember ye the law of Moses, my servant,*" left on record an injunction for after centuries, and for all people, that the Mosaic Code was never to be abrogated or superceded, but to be held in sacred trust and carried down generation after generation to the end of time.

It would be superfluous to refer here to the numerous Psalms which demonstrate how entirely their authors were imbued with the doctrine that the Mosaic dispensation was imperishable, and indeed it would be worse than futile to adduce any arguments therefrom, since these compositions, admirable though they are, not being inspired like the Books of the Prophets, merely serve to convey the individual belief of the writers, and, therefore, fail to afford that positive evidence which alone could give to their words the authoritative stamp of truth.

Having sought to show beyond all question that the laws of Moses are to endure "for ever," and admitting that had this assertion been qualified by the admission that some portion only of those laws, particularly the Ten Commandments, were given in perpetuity, the arguments here advanced would have met with little opposition, if not, indeed, with universal assent, it now becomes essential to offer a few brief remarks on this subject, and endeavour to prove that the *whole* Mosaic Code is immutable, and must stand or fall in its integrity. Most certainly it is impossible to find one single verse or sentence in the Pentateuch wherein it can be said that Moses ever broached the thought of the slightest repeal or change, or wherein he specified any difference in regard to the divers laws he taught the people, except, indeed, in those instances where their performance were only possible so long as the Israelites inhabited the Holy Land, as, for example, the law of manslaughter in connection with the cities of refuge; the sacrifices and burnt offerings in the Sanctuary of the Holy of Holies; the jubilee and such ordinances as solely appertained to agriculture, the all engrossing occupation of those times, and nearly the only means of subsistence or prosperity.

Now, can it be doubted that had not every law been equally binding, the distinction would have been plainly set forth, and the obligation of each especial statute been clearly defined in that Pentateuch which was, at the command of God, to be handed down from father to son, and preserved unimpaired to all futurity? And happily, such has been the case for long centuries; indeed, had not the Mosaic religion, with the sublime ethical precepts it unfolds, been intended to abide " for everlasting," the Jewish nation must long, long ere this have become extinct, trampled down as it has been by unceasing and cruel persecutions, oppressed and oftentimes gravitating to its fall through incessant struggles for bare existence, and, withal, vigorously and often ruthlessly assailed by the intolerant and bigoted followers of new-born creeds, who, in the search for proselytes and religious supremacy, ignored the stem from which they had sprung, and forgetful of the infallibility and perfection of God's laws, enunciated for their own belief a higher—a more philanthropic code of morality! Truly, the fact that Judaism has stood firm and majestic through long ages, and its Sinaic laws been preserved intact for centuries, must of itself afford ample guarantee of its permanent duration; but, further, let it once be proved that those laws are "true and perfect altogether," thus worthy of being perpetuated, and more than enough will have been advanced in support of the assurance conveyed through the Holy Volume, that the law of Moses was destined to be transmitted from "generation to generation," from "everlasting to everlasting," "for evermore."

The words "true" and "perfect" now demand our attention, and these having the closest affinity when considered in reference to the law of Moses, may therefore be treated in common, for it is self-evident that this code could not be perfect unless the whole of its component parts

—its very essence—were true, whilst, on the other hand, it must be true, since it proceeds from the Omniscient, the God of truth. These emphatic and all comprehensive words have also this in unison, that they admit of no superlative, for what is true cannot be more true, or that which is perfect, cannot, by any possibility, attain to a greater degree of perfection. But it may be said that the words "true" and "perfect" are supple, and oftentimes change their character altogether, according to times and circumstances, and this may be justly affirmed when human institutions are in question; but can such be advanced in regard to those laws which were given by the immutable Lord of all flesh? Assuredly not; we may not, we dare not, entertain even the mere notion, while, indeed, none but a sceptic will deny that the Mosaic Code —unaltered,—unchanged,—is as true and perfect now as at the period of its delivery on Mount Sinai.

It would be worse than useless further to allude to what appears so self-evident, except for the fact that it is repeatedly alleged and strenuously contended that the new dispensation of another creed has introduced laws and doctrines calculated to teach a higher morality, as well as a purer spirituality, and therefore should supersede the old; but such being the case, it becomes imperative on us to examine if this assertion could have any solid foundation, for if it were possible to prove that even one of the Mosaic laws needed to be supplanted or supplemented, then would the heavenly-given code necessarily be imperfect. To amend that which is perfect is manifestly impossible, since any change made is simply to render it imperfect.

Now did the Sinaic dispensation lack that vital principle which is fitted to ensure the happiness of all God's creatures, did not the various laws enjoin virtue and tend to repress vice, in a word, did they not inculcate the highest possible morality consistent with human nature, then, indeed, might the Jewish code be considered ill adapted for that standard of perfection to which all mankind should look up for guidance, and thereby seek to gain the favour of a kind and merciful Judge, the gracious giver of the Holy Law. But as it can be amply demonstrated that the Mosaic code fulfils all these conditions, the conclusion which ensues is inevitable, that, taking the words true and perfect in their literal signification, without any double interpretation, they clearly define the character of God's sublime law, and as "true" and "perfect" it will surely endure in its entirety from "everlasting to everlasting."

It now only remains to advert to some few of the numerous facts and inferences which lead to the conviction, indeed to the certainty, that the Mosaic code is alike true and perfect, and among them the following may well be selected:—Firstly. That it directly emanated from the Divine Will, and moreover was solemnly delivered by the Supreme himself, the Lord of infinite wisdom and perfection, and in the presence of a vast assembled multitude, as we read in Deut. ch. 29, v. 10.: "Ye stand this day all of you before the Lord your God; your captains of your tribes, your elders, your little ones, your wives, and the stranger that is in your camp, from the hewer of wood unto the drawer of thy water, that thou should'st enter into covenant with the Lord thy God unto his oath which the Lord thy God maketh with thee this day;" and proceeding to verse 15, we find it there clearly and amply demonstrated that it was not intended to be either local or temporary, but was adapted for transmission to all futurity, else it would not have been thus enjoined, "Neither with you only who stand here this day do I make this covenant and this oath; *but also with him that is not here this day.*"

Secondly: The distinct command given that there should be no amendment or alteration whatsoever to the Law, is of itself alone proof positive that it contains all the elements essential and vital to man's well-being. And this is the injunction, Deut. ch. 4, v. 2, "Ye shall not add unto the word which I command you, nor shall ye diminish aught from it," and again at ch. 12, v. 32, "What thing soever I command you, observe to do it; thou shalt not add thereto nor diminish from it."

Thirdly: Its duration, for it could not possibly have resisted the repeated attacks levelled against it from all sides during no less a period than thirty centuries and survived unmaimed and vigorous, but that it derived a vitality which truth and perfection alone could impart, or in the words of Moses, Deut. ch. 4, v. 8, "What nation has statutes so righteous as all this law?" Had it lacked any essential precepts or ordinances, had some command calculated to lead man to virtue and to God been omitted, its stability would surely have been endangered, but that it has weathered every storm, and during the lapse of ages seen many a new conflicting system rise and fall, assuredly speaks in a marvellous and unparalleled manner the perfection and truth of the immortal code propounded by our inspired Prophet.

Fourthly: The Laws themselves with their high moral inculcations, their applicability to every situation of life, to every phase of existence, from tenderest youth to old age, their adaptation to each lofty aspiration, each spiritual want; in a word, their potency in ministering to the happiness and well-being of humanity, affords conclusive evidence that they are of Divine origin, and hence must infallibly be alike true and perfect.

It would, however, be as inopportune as superfluous, to enlarge here on this subject, since it will be the purport of the two following chapters practically to demonstrate in detail all that has just been advanced in regard to the

Mosaic Code in its entirety. Suffice it to remark that therein the sacred rights of life and property are strictly prescribed; forbearance, charity, love, and the purest spirit of philanthropy are enjoined; every virtue is inculcated, and the duty of man to his God and to his fellow creatures is clearly demonstrated and emphatically enforced, whilst it may also be observed that God Himself hath said to His people, Deut. ch. 18, v. 13. "Be perfect," a command which taken in conjunction with the Divine decree then delivered by Infinite Wisdom and goodness, is a further confirmation of the declaration that "the law is perfect and righteous altogether." By the observance of the Heaven-given code alone can man hope to become "perfect," since assuredly conscience and judgment would of themselves be alike powerless to direct him aright or map out moral excellence, truth, and perfection.

Fifthly: The effect of the Mosaic Code on individual character. The world's history most certainly contains no more perfect, no more righteous men than those who took the Sinaic laws for their guidance and strictly followed their sublime ethical inculcations. To their rigid adherence to each precept, each command, in the dispensation vouchsafed from Heaven, may surely be traced the excellence which distinguished each true, each faithful servant of God, nor indeed does this remark refer exclusively to Biblical characters, such for example as Moses himself, or Samuel, Daniel, or Jeremiah, but is clearly discernible in the lives of every individual who has made himself a name for goodness, for probity and for intrinsic worth.

Sixthly: The bias of the Sinaic laws on the human mind. That men of the greatest intellectual powers and towering mental calibre have in succeeding generations regarded those laws as the very basis of all excellence is not without its significance, for were they not alike true and perfect, they would surely have failed to maintain their ascendency and have ceased to be transmitted as a glorious heirloom from father to son. But it is beyond dispute that the very men who have shone brightest and displayed the most exalted moral qualities, as well as the highest mental culture, are those who have borne undying testimony both by word and deed to their profound appreciation of the Divine commands. Did not King David proclaim their efficacy when he said—"Thy word is a lamp to my feet and a light unto my path"? And again, Ps. ch. 19, v. 7, "The law of the Lord is perfect, converting the soul: the word of the Lord is pure, enlightening the eyes." Further, he declared, "Thy commandment is exceedingly broad; for ever, O Lord, thy word is settled in heaven; give me understanding and I shall keep thy law, yea, I shall keep it with my whole heart." That he sought to perpetuate these statutes, believing in their perfection and adaptation to every human want, we may feel assured, when we regard his dying injunction to the son who was to succeed him on the throne. In 1 Kings ch. 2, v. 3, we read, "David charged Solomon, saying, Keep the charge of the Lord thy God to walk in his ways, to keep his statutes and his commandments and his judgments *as it is written in the law of Moses.*" Nor did King Solomon, the wisest of men, hold them in less estimation, judging by his writings in general and by the following injunction in particular—Eccles. ch. 12, v. 13, "Fear God *and keep his commandments*, for this is the whole duty of man." Also in the most solemn and emphatic manner did each sacred penman extol them, and with a zealous fervour exhort their performance, whilst they further sought to transmit them in their integrity to after generations. And none more earnestly laboured therein than Ezra, the "ready scribe of the Law of Moses, who "prepared his heart to seek the law of the Lord," who "opened the Book of the Lord in the sight of the people and caused them to understand the sense thereof." Even the very last injunction of the last of the Prophets shows the law was held in no less estimation after the lapse of 1,300 years, since it was enjoined by Malachi ch. 4, v. 4, "*Remember ye the law of Moses*, with the statutes and judgments."

It is not necessary here to allude specifically to the host of distinguished men of more modern times whose writings and acts alike bear testimony to their belief in the perfection of the Mosaic Code, since their names will for ever be found engraven on the page of profane History.*

Seventhly: The laws being free from all ambiguity and obscurity, they admit of, indeed

---

* See chapter V. which treats on this subject.

even court, the keenest enquiry. Their simplicity, being without a shadow of mysticism, permit the test of the severest criticism, and withal, the profound wisdom which lies at their very root, never fails to manifest itself at each important juncture, triumphing over those laws and observances, which have been fashioned by fallible man, and thereby giving positive evidence of their truth and perfection.

Eighth and lastly: The fact that no one command clashes with another, but all dovetail with the most admirable precision, and together form a bulwark of moral ethics to which each of God's creatures may resort for guidance, and in those true and righteous laws find that which Infinite Wisdom decreed should be the only, the undeviating rule of life and of moral conduct.

Chapter II.

The Laws themselves now call for special and separate consideration, and it will be the main purport of this and the following chapter to substantiate what has been advanced, and show how fully they bear the imprint of infinite wisdom and justice, those high and gracious attributes of the Supreme Ruler of the Universe. With this object we shall summarize and bring into prominent relief some of the many eminently practical Laws which the inspired penman drew up and clearly set forth in the Pentateuch for the guidance of after generations.

It being, however, advisable to consider the varied covenants and laws under two distinct headings, it will now be our object to pass briefly in review those ordinances which few but the sceptic and the scoffer will impugn or disregard, postponing to the following chapter our comments on such Divine injunctions as possibly display less markedly the high and important influence they are calculated to exercise on the world at large and on the Jewish nation in particular.

On directing then our attention, firstly, to those laws and ordinances, most of which have not been prized by the Jewish people alone, but also by the enlightened and pious of every civilized nation, it will be well to commence with the consideration of the ten commandments, the very basis of moral ethics, embracing as they do the whole duty of man to God and to his fellow-creatures. But the all-comprehensive precepts which are embodied in the Decalogue will demand separately only a few brief remarks, since they may be left to speak their own perfection and Divine origin.

Taking in conjuction the first and second commandments, both of which distinctly proclaim the Unity of the Godhead in the sentences, "I am the Lord thy God" and "Thou shalt have no other God besides me," then coupling them with the emphatic, clear and oft repeated declaration, "The Lord is ONE," and "I, the Lord am Holy," it must be admitted that these two commandments are well calculated to subserve a high moral purpose, since they tend to fix the mind exclusively on the sole fount of Infinite goodness and holiness, and greatly conduce to rouse the best sentiments of the heart, and direct them in all purity of spirit to the One immutable Being to whom alone is due all reverence, all love, all obedience, or, in a word, that faithful adherence to the inculcations of righteousness which are so strictly, so solemnly enjoined in the all-gracious statutes and ordinances vouchsafed from on High.

Turning to the third commandment, we cannot fail to discern that in order to act in accordance with it, we should always collect our thoughts before we utter the ineffable name of God in prayer, for to neglect this bounden duty must infallibly lead to the disregard of what is due to the Supreme, whose " mercies are new every morning," and will surely end in our " taking the Lord's name in vain." Further remarks we reserve till treating on the ninth commandment, when this injunction will be considered in its social bearing.

Proceeding then to the fourth commandment, it will not be needful to make any comments on its first ordinance, " to labour and do all thy work" during six days, as even ordinary experience clearly demonstrates that social well-being depends in a great measure on each individual accomplishing his allotted duties and sedulously fulfilling his especial vocation, but we must briefly dilate on the solemn mandate of the Supreme, "to rest on the seventh day," a command repeatedly and emphatically enjoined throughout the Pentateuch, since the beautiful institution of the Sabbath and the beneficial effects its observance is calculated to produce, are only too frequently disregarded or ignored. This injunction, however, having been considered in all its bearings under the heading of "The Sabbath" in "Moral Biblical Gleanings" (the author's last religious work), it will here suffice to give such extracts therefrom as especially refer to the subject matter in question. "Among the benefits which it should bring in its train may be numbered bodily and mental refreshment; and for this we must know nothing of idleness, but much of repose. On this day, a day of compensation, lost stamina is to be recovered, power to be restored, energies to be recruited, the weary brain relaxed, and mental quietude engendered by calm, healthy and truthful reflections. When this result is attained, we shall be able to resume with all necessary energy the business engagements of the ensuing week, and efficiently discharge the many obligations and duties which pertain to our position in life. Renewed zest will have been engendered by the temporary suspension of business cares, and the mind, having for a time buried in oblivion thoughts which worried or oppressed it, will have regained its elasticity, its vigor, and with them renewed confidence and trust. The next benefit we may derive from the sacred day of rest is intellectual improvement, for does not the Bible tell us that 'they who seek the Lord understand all things?' That mind will be clear and bright to discern the things of earth which has been furnished with heavenly truths, and if these be not taken to heart on the peaceful Sabbath, they will assuredly receive little attention on the working days. . . . Finally, a benefit which greatly depends thereon is our moral progress; a truly pious and virtuous character is not to be formed without those reflections which the holy day is every way calculated to suggest. We must then learn to *be* and to *do* good; we must turn our thoughts inwards, examine the disposition of our heart, review our past conduct, give heed to errors committed, and fixedly determine the straight line for future guidance. When reflections followed by good resolutions have been made a constant weekly practice, then shall we be well fitted to take an active part in the business and charities of life." . . . "But would we enhance our appreciation of that Sabbath which does so much to promote our worldly interests and confers on us so many spiritual benefits, we have only for a moment to consider this heavenly boon *withdrawn*, and that we were obliged to toil mind and body without respite. Would not our constitution be undermined, and our health greatly impaired? Would not debility and illness attack our frames, force us from the haunts of men, and injure our worldly prospects? Would not our thoughts gradually centre in the things of earth to the exclusion of our spiritual welfare, and our hearts harden under the never-ceasing stimulus of selfish interests? There would, indeed, be little left to sanctify our lives; we should only at rare intervals, and for short periods, raise our minds to our Maker, study His laws, and so frame our conduct thereby. Truly both our moral and physical well-being would have received a rude shock." . . . " Let us therefore have ever before our eyes its negative as well as its positive advantages, and love the holy Sabbath with its ordinances for its own sake as well as for the good it can and will accomplish. We shall then take for its motto—rest, trust and be thankful—bearing ever in mind that to disregard the beautiful provisions of Providence is to work against our own well-being, and to violate the Sabbatical appointment is truly a suicidal act."

The fifth commandment, the sense of which is thus reiterated in Lev. ch. 19, v. 3, in these words—"Ye shall fear every man his father and his mother,"—may also be dismissed with a brief notice, since the injunction to honour and obey the authors of our being, through whom, under Providence, we have from infancy received every enjoyable blessing, appeals directly to each human breast, and assuredly none but those who are utterly dead to right feeling and generous emotions will disregard it. Being unwilling, however, to pass over this command without showing that, like every

Divine law, it must not only be fraught with material benefit to those who adhere to its inculcations, but also that its neglect will surely entail the most dire consequences, we deem it advisable to contrast the effects which can hardly fail to attend the fulfilment or non-fulfilment of a son's imperative duty. And for this purpose we will once more give a brief extract from " Moral Biblical Gleanings," referring the reader to the heading of " Filial Affection," for a full treatment of the subject. " The youth who attends to the admonitions of his fond parents, hearkens respectfully to their advice, and follows it cheerfully, ever striving to walk by the greater light of their experience, and seeking to become deserving of their glowing aspirations, will prove himself a worthy son; and never yet did a worthy son fail in performing his part in life worthily as a man. Earnestly fulfilling every moral duty, he will assuredly secure the respect and love of all good men, and the happiness which smiled upon him first within his home will go forth with him into the world without." . . . " Truly filial affection is not alone a duty, but a prerogative; and thrice happy the son who can throw so glowing and glorious a halo over the spirit of a dying parent, receiving in return what must spread a hallowed joy over his entire life—that loving parent's parting benediction." . . . "But heavy and severe will be the penalty which that youth has to pay, who, regardless of duty and his own self-interest, rashly and wilfully disobeys parental commands. Surely, if every minor dereliction of duty is fraught with evil, sad and painful must be the consequences entailed by filial disobedience. To him who refuses the light of experience, the road to ruin will be as swift as certain. Heart, purse, and health, will soon be alike bankrupt. When conscience ceases to struggle for the right, when no chord of sympathy or love is struck by the sight of anguish written in legible characters on that face which it was a son's duty to irradiate with joy, when a father's anger is obdurately defied, and passion is allowed full sway, that goal is nearly reached whence there can be no return. Truly nought but compunction of conscience will be left to him who, besides ruining his own prospects, has disappointed the fond aspirations of loving parents. Nor can his sorrow be otherwise than greatly heightened when he sees death laying its cold hand on that father or mother to whom all reparation has now become impossible. Yet even a severer sting than this will occasionally wound the undutiful child; for if his unfilial conduct has inflicted a blow which in any measure hastened that fatal end, an agony of remorse and self-condemnation will steal upon him; too late will he then remember that parents forgive much, very much; indeed, that the fond mother will pardon nearly all but ingratitude, and that by obstinately persisting in subjecting her to this cruel wrong, he has basely stabbed her to the quick — perhaps broken her heart, and sent her sorrowing to the grave. Let, then, the son who would save himself in later years from the stings of conscience and much bitter grief, beware of making his first step in opposition to a parent's counsel. Indeed, it surely behoves him to regard such advice as an inestimable boon, for then will he make a pleasure of obedience, and wisely profiting by the experience of age and the lessons of love, will become an honour to his family, a pride and a joy to beloved and loving parents."

To the last five commandments have we now to direct our attention, and these prohibitory laws may not only be considered together, but can advantageously be taken in conjunction with the all-comprehensive and sublime ethical precept—Lev. ch. 19, v. xviii., to "love thy neighbour as thyself," in which they are clearly comprised. And here it may be worthy of remark, lest the idea conveyed by the term "neighbour"* might be regarded in its narrow and contracted sense, that the Hebrew word should, according to the ablest Jewish scholars, be translated "fellow-man," and further, we find the significant expression "stranger" introduced in the almost synonimous sentence—Deut. ch. 10, v. xix., "The Lord of lords loveth the stranger, *love ye therefore the stranger,*" which imparts a distinct and definite idea to the mind, thereby precluding all misinterpretation, all misconception. In these injunctions, containing the very essence and embodiment of Judaism, are to be found a

---

* In regard to this word "neighbour" it is worthy of remark that no one verse is to be found restricting it to an Israelite, indeed it is practically demonstrated otherwise, since the term—neighbour—was equally applied to the Adullamite and to the Egyptian.

deterrent to such sinful propensities as must surely lead to the infringement, if not indeed to the positive infraction of the last five commandments, which have an especial bearing upon the duty of man to man. Let us but truly "Love our neighbour," and it will necessarily follow that we shall resolutely refrain from injuring him even under provocation, or in any way wounding his feelings by either word or act; indeed, the pure spirit of benevolence, or charity in its broadest sense, will certainly characterize our conduct and keep us ever mindful of the rights and interests of others.

Now assuredly it is owing to the wilful violation of the sixth commandment—" Thou shalt not kill," as well as of the grand fundamental principle to "love thy neighbour as thyself," that duelling is yet rampant on the continent of Europe, and that so many descend to their graves branded with the curse of Cain. Also, when we slander or take away the reputation of a fellow-creature, so that ruin and misery ensue, then are we but too surely shortening, even if not cutting, the very thread of life, and further, we are breaking the eighth commandment; for unjustly to detract from a man's merit or honour and lower him in the world's esteem through untruthful statements or calumny, is simply to "steal" from "our neighbour" that which we never afterwards can fully restore, or for which it is impossible to make adequate reparation even by a formal open recantation.

Then as to the seventh commandment, what do the annals of the Divorce Court prove but the constant transgression of the Divine injunction forbidding conjugal infidelity, and that the Law given "for our good always" being once broken and a breach made in the family circle, misery and disgrace speedily follow. And truly, if we love not the one who is nearest and should be dearest to us, how may we hope to "love the stranger" or any denizen of the outer world whether a "neighbour" or an "alien"?

The eighth commandment in its broad signification needs no special remarks here, since only the utterly worthless and abandoned are capable of the act of stealing; but as regards the many deceptions generally termed "tricks of the trade," which are most certainly a species of theft, we shall treat of them when considering the ordinance that emphatically denounces and prohibits the use of "false weights and measures." Again, what could be more at variance with the injunction to love our fellow-man than to break the ninth commandment, and " bear false witness against our neighbour," for to do so clearly betokens some sinister motive, a cruel animosity and rancorous feeling that nothing could justify, while it also shows a criminal perversity in daring to disregard the third commandment and " take God's name in vain." But all further allusion to so heinous, so iniquitous a violation of a solemn duty and sacred obligation is here quite unnecessary, since every-day experience amply demonstrates that honour and truth are the pillars on which depend and rest the well-being of the entire social fabric ; withdraw these supports to moral rectitude and assuredly all would soon be utter chaos.

Finally, in regard to the tenth commandment, it is evident that by no possibility could we violate the solemn injunction, not to covet any possession which belongs to another, if we had at heart the sublime precept to " love thy neighbour as thyself." It is indeed pure selfishness which produces that inordinate desire, that restless craving which begins in covetousness and but too surely ends in envy and discontent, the two greatest and most insidious foes to all enjoyment, all happiness. That a disregard of this warning against cupidity and unruly passions will involve the very worst consequences is only too certain, while it cannot fail to lead to the infraction of other Divine ordinances promulgated at Sinai.

Now although the last five prohibitory commandments taken in conjunction with the grand Mosaic precept to "love thy neighbour as thyself" indicate and define, with the most marvellous simplicity and clearness, the high moral duties which are incumbent on man in relation to his fellow-man, nevertheless there are further numerous supplementary injunctions to be found in the Pentateuch which breathe alike the purest spirit of philanthropy and brotherly love, and thence being in perfect, in absolute harmony with the ennobling teachings of the Decalogue, give them yet additional force and significance.*

---

* It is truly astonishing that any one conversant with the ethical teachings of the Great Sovereign, can overlook the fact that the sublime injunction to "love thy neighbour (fellow creature) as thyself" was not only

And to demonstrate this we will now cite some few of the many beneficial laws and statutes which the Omniscient, in His infinite love and mercy, ordained and declared obligatory on each of His creatures as being all-powerful to promote and ultimately ensure individual happiness and universal good.

Directing our attention, firstly, to those ordinances which bear the closest affinity to the fundamental principle of action inculcated in the Mosaic code to love our fellow-creature, whether he be native born or an alien, the following verses may well be selected for consideration: Ex. ch. 23, v. i., "Thou shalt not raise a false report; put not thine hand with the wicked to be an unrighteous witness," and Lev. ch. 19, v. xvi., "Thou shalt not go up and down as a tale-bearer among thy people;" thus showing that neither directly nor indirectly are we to asperse or undermine the reputation

inculcated by Moses, but was made the cardinal doctrine, the very essence of his moral code. Nevertheless, as only too many men of another creed, through a strange fatuity or blindness, credit the New Testament with being the first exponent of this precept, it behoves the Jew not to permit this erroneous impression to pass unchallenged, but ever seek to give expression to this fundamental principle of Mosaicism both by word and deed.

of any one, a proceeding which can only be dictated by rancour, revenge, or some other evil passion, and which is totally at variance with the sublime command to "love thy neighbour as thyself." Then we read in Lev. ch. 24, *v.* xxii., "Ye shall have one manner of law as well *for the stranger* as for one of your own country," and the tenor of this command is still more emphatically enjoined in Num. ch. 15, *v.* xv-xvi., "One ordinance shall be both for you and also for the stranger that sojourneth with you, an ordinance for ever in your generations; as ye are, so shall the stranger be before the Lord. One law and one manner shall be for you and the stranger that sojourneth with you;" also in Ex. ch. 22, *v.* xxi., "Thou shalt not vex a stranger or oppress him; ye shall not afflict any widow or fatherless child," thus coupling the stranger with the unprotected and poor of the land. And again in Deut. ch. 24, *v.* xiv., "Thou shalt not oppress a hired servant, whether he be one of thy brethren or a stranger." And this is also enjoined in the fourth commandment, wherein it is decreed that "the stranger" should do no manner of work on the Sabbath day. Again in Deut. ch. 15

v. xi., "Thou shalt open thy hand wide unto thy brother and to the needy," here likewise inferring the stranger, as also in the following verse, "Lev. ch. 19, *v.* xiii., "The wages of him that is hired" (mostly *prisoners of war*, and therefore aliens) "shall not abide with thee all night until the morning," and this is repeated in Lev. ch. 25, *v.* xxxv., "If thy brother be waxen poor and fallen into decay, then thou shalt relieve him; yea, *though he be a stranger* or a sojourner; that he may live with thee;" and again in Deut. ch. 24, *v.* xvii., "Thou shalt not pervert the judgment of the stranger, nor of the fatherless, nor take a widow's raiment to pledge." Nor is the respect due to old age ignored, for we are bidden in Lev. 19, *v.* xxxii., to "rise up before the hoary head and honor the face of the old man."

And now we would revert more particularly to some few of the admirable and eminently practical laws which have for object to hold man to the performance of all that is strictly just and honourable in his dealings with his fellow-man, and to restrain him from the indulgence of that cupidity or individual greed of gain which will surely lead to misery and to shame. To select a few of the most important, we begin with the command in Lev. ch. 19, v. xxxv., "Thou shalt do no unrighteousness," and to make this injunction the more emphatic, the more stringent, the words "I am the Lord thy God" are added. And next, Lev. ch. 9, v. xi., "Thou shalt not deal falsely one with another; thou shalt not defraud thy neighbour." Again, Lev. ch. 25, v. xiv., "If thou sell ought unto thy neighbour, or buyest ought of thy neighbour's hand, ye shall not oppress one another." Also in Deut. ch. 25, v. xiii., "Thou shalt not have in thy bag divers weights, a great and a small, thou shalt not have in thy house divers measures, a great and a small, but thou shalt have a perfect and just weight, a perfect and just measure shalt thou have." That these laws are frequently evaded or ignored even in the present advanced state of civilisation, is only too patent to those who give due heed to the several reprehensible methods adopted for the purpose of securing additional and illegitimate profits through what has been termed "tricks of the trade." The sensational mode of puffing wares for sale, the deception practised by means of ticketing up apparently low and attractive prices, indistinct figures being coupled with other dark ones, the adulteration of food, now so loudly denounced, also the system of overcharging by means of selling one specified quality and quantity, whilst substituting them and really delivering a lesser measurement or an inferior article, together with other hardly less culpable artifices, better concealed, perhaps, but all in contravention to that fairness and honesty which is so emphatically enjoined in the Heaven-given code. Again we are commanded in the following injunction not to be extortionate or to press hard upon such of our fellow men as need our assistance, Ex. ch. 22, v. xxv., "If thou lend money to any of my people that is poor, thou shalt not be to him as a usurer, neither shalt thou lay upon him usury. If thou at all take thy neighbour's raiment to pledge, thou shalt deliver it unto him by that the sun goeth down;" and in Lev. ch. 25, v. xxxvii., "Thou shalt not give unto thy brother if he be waxen poor, yea, though he be a stranger or a sojourner, thy money upon usury, nor lend him thy victuals for increase." And be it here observed in reference to this latter subject, that the true interpretation of the

Hebrew word is not "usury" but "interest," or a fair compensation for some voluntary loan (see Dr. H. Adler's admirable pamphlet on "Usury"), and even this was only to be permitted when it was advanced for mercantile purposes. This subject, however, needs no further comment here, since it will again have attention in the following chapter.

But the Mosaic system goes much further than the inculcation of mere fairness and honesty of purpose in all our dealings, for therein we find the most distinct, the most emphatic call on our active, practical benevolence. We are not simply enjoined to do our fellow-man no wrong, we are bidden to do him positive good. Thus it is commanded to give in charity one-tenth of the wealth with which we have been blessed. Deut. ch. 14. *v.* xxxviii., "At the end of three years thou shalt bring forth all the tithe of thine increase, and the Levite and the stranger, and the fatherless, and the widow, shall come and shall eat and be satisfied." And again, *v.* xxii., "Thou shalt *truly* tithe all the increase of thy seed, that the field bringeth forth year by year, that thou mayest learn to fear the Lord thy God always," and were this Divine behest duly carried out in practice, penury with its too frequent concomitants, misery and crime, would be almost unknown! The sublime institution of the Sabbatical year had the same purpose, serving to lessen destitution and preclude oppressive exactions. All who had fallen might hope to regain their high estate and become once more independent. Alienation of property in perpetuity was rendered impossible, while it also entailed the remission of debts owing by the poor and the manumission of the slave. And here are the several injunctions in regard to its observance. Ex. ch. 23, *v.* x., " Six years thou shalt sow thy land, and shalt gather in the fruits thereof, but the seventh year thou shalt let it rest and lie still, that the poor of thy people may eat, and what they leave the beasts of the field shall eat." This is repeated again and again in Leviticus, with the following addition, at ch. 23, v. xxii., " Thou shalt not gather any gleaning of thy harvest : thou shalt leave them *unto the poor and to the stranger ;* I am the Lord your God." Further, we have in Deut. ch. 15, *v.* i., " At the end of every seven years *thou shalt make a release;* every creditor that lendeth ought unto his neighbour shall release it, he shall not exact it." And again, Lev. ch. 25, *v.* viii., " Thou shalt number seven sabbaths of years unto thee, seven times seven years, and ye shall hallow the fiftieth year and proclaim liberty throughout all the land, it shall be a jubilee unto you, and *ye shall return every man unto his possession.*" Then again, what could possibly be more mild, more beneficent, than the following ordinances which inculcate true charity, forbearance, sympathy and love? Deut. ch. 15, *v.* viii., " Thou shalt not harden thy heart, nor shut thine hand from thy poor brother, but thou shalt open thy hand *wide* unto him, and shall surely lend him sufficient for his need in that which he wanteth ;" and this is repeated at *v.* xi., " Thou shalt open thy hand wide unto thy brother, to the poor and to the needy in the land," implying the stranger. Again in Lev. ch. 25, *v.* xiv., " If thou sell ought unto thy neighbour, or buyest ought of thy neighbour's hand, ye shall not oppress one another." Then in regard to the Temple worship, it is ordained, Deut. ch. 18, *v.* iv., that "The first fruits also of thy corn, of thy wine, and of thy oil, and the first of the fleece of thy sheep, shalt thou give to the Levite, Thou shalt be perfect with the Lord thy God." Further, there is a species of fairness due even to dumb animals which has not been overlooked, and various are the injunctions in the Pentateuch inculcating their kindly treatment. Merciful indeed are the commands, Lev. ch. 22, v. xxviii., "Whether it be cow or ewe, ye shall not kill it and her young both in one day," and to like effect, Ex. ch. 34, v. xxvi., "Thou shalt not seethe a kid in his mother's milk." Again, Deut. ch. 22, v. iv., "Thou shalt not see thy brother's ass or his ox fall down by the way and hide thyself from them." And v. x., "Thou shalt not plow with an ox and an ass together." Also, ch. 25, v. iv., "Thou shalt not muzzle the ox when he treadeth out the corn." Then we are bidden to give rest to the beast of burden on the Sabbath day: to slaughter the animals granted us for food in the speediest and most merciful manner: to let the poor bird go free: whilst other ordinances, equally beneficent, all incontrovertibly prove that to compassionate the brute creation is the fixed law, the essential principle of Judaism.

We will now conclude with the consideration

of those injunctions which seem to appeal more directly to the individual than to the whole social body, but which are as surely calculated to ensure its permanent benefit as they are to secure the well-being of each member constituting it. Among the most important commands assuredly rank those which inculcate the duty of parents to instruct their offspring and keep God's laws constantly before them. We read in Deut. ch. 11, *v*. xix., "Ye shall teach them (these my words) to your children, speaking of them when thou sittest in thine house and when thou walkest by the way," implying, indeed, on every suitable occasion. A youth thus brought up can hardly fail to become a good man and a blessing to the parents who have trained him in this pious manner. The ordinances for the observance of the Festivals we find in Lev. ch. 23, *v*. vii., "These are the feasts of the Lord, even *holy convocations*, ye shall do no servile work therein," again repeated in Numbers ch. 28, *v*. xviii., and well calculated are they not only to promote social and friendly intercourse, but also to uproot the seeds of discord and strife, while tending to draw us nearer to God, either through a sense of gratitude for memorable mercies vouchsafed in the long, long past, or the fulfilment of some golden hope, some heavenly-promised boon. And the above remark is peculiarly applicable to the solemn day of Atonement, so beautiful in its very simplicity. It tells us we must forgive before we may hope to be forgiven, and were this consideration fully recognized, no feud, no quarrel could last more than one year, for this hallowed day would bring healing on its wings, and whilst asking God's pardon with heartfelt contrition, no unkind feelings towards a fellow creature would harbour in our breasts; past enmity and ill-will would surely sink back into oblivion.

It can hardly be necessary here to make more than a passing allusion to the statutes concerning abstinence from certain food; take for example the following: Lev. ch. 11, *v.* iv., repeated at Deut. ch. 14, *v.* iii., "Thou shalt not eat any abominable thing. They that chew the cud but divide not the hoof are unclean unto you, and the swine,* ye shall not eat of their

---

* It can but be a matter of surprise that while many of the ablest scientific men of the day hold in high estimation the sanitary laws of Moses and give free expression to their opinion, nevertheless they seem in a great

flesh. Of all clean birds ye may eat, but every creeping thing is unclean unto you," also in Ex. ch. 22, *v.* xxxi,, "Ye shall be holy unto me; neither shall ye eat any flesh that is torn of beasts in the field," since it has been proved to demonstration that the dietary laws of Moses have been fruitful of good to the people for whom they were especially instituted, while the

measure to overlook or disregard those dietary prohibitions which most certainly have no less a claim to their especial notice and appreciation. All who have given their attention to this subject will assuredly certify that they who partake freely of any food pronounced unclean by the Mosaic statutes become subject to many of the most grievous diseases which afflict humanity. But if we might be permitted to single out one unclean animal which demonstrates more clearly than another how important is the observance of the prohibitory laws in regard to food, we should not hesitate to name the hog, which ever wallowing in the mire, rejects no refuse, howsoever foul or impure, in the endeavour to satiate its gross and gluttonous appetite, and thence will not unfrequently be found to generate those subtle and venomous juices which taint its flesh and render it totally unfit for human consumption. To instance how deadly poisonous the flesh of the swine may become, we here give an outline of a sad and painful occurrence which was graphically described quite recently by a trustworthy daily paper. On board the barque ———— a cask of pork was opened, and a portion was boiled into soup, of which fourteen sailors partook, all of whom soon became seriously ill and grew worse day by day, till at the end of a fortnight, after much suffering, some went raving mad and others died in horrible agony, whilst four alone survived, and even their health was materially undermined.

infraction of them has at all times been pregnant with evil consequences. Truly, when it is considered that the Omniscient, in His goodness, not only has declared what food is clean, therefore wholesome and calculated to promote health and strength, but has also specified what is *unclean*, or gross and pernicious alike to physical and mental vigour, it is surprising that any single individual should run counter to the explicit command of God in regard to this matter, and partake of those species of diet which have been so clearly, so strictly forbidden. But these hygienic laws even serve yet another beneficial purpose, since they impose a restraint on the appetite. Abstinence from certain classes of food greatly tends to give a power of control over our sensual nature, and which, if only turned to good account, will enable us to curb all gluttonous propensities and any undue craving after luxuries.

The laws referring to some of the most important ceremonial rites also need but brief comment, since no true Israelite could by any possibility neglect their observance. Regarding, firstly, the Abrahamic covenant, it will suffice to draw attention to what an able writer of the

Christian faith has said on the subject, and for which reference may be made to the *Lancet* of the 16th January, 1875, where it is proved to demonstration that the observance of this Divine injunction is ever pregnant with the most sanitary and salutary effects. As to the Mezuzots to be placed on the door-posts as commanded in Deut. ch. 1, v. xx., and the Tsisith to be worn on the person according to the command in Numbers ch. 15, v. xxxviii., it is enough to say that they are simply signs to meet our gaze and keep us constantly in remembrance of God and His holy laws, or in other words, outward aids to draw us to pious reflection at suitable intervals, and most certainly possessing no other talismanic virtue. Not a single rite commanded from on High suggests the slightest notion of the existence of any supernatural power, or in the remotest degree contains aught of mysticism; each one has solely for object to assist the worship of the heart, while under no possible circumstance are they intended to weaken or supercede it.

We now come to the subject of the priests' dress, and clearly are the proper sacerdotal habiliments specified in the 28th chapter of

Exodus. That the description of special vestments to be worn by ministers should thus be distinctly defined proves how highly important it is that they who officiate in a Temple of worship should be above the vanity which indulges in decorations according to individual caprice, and through so questionable a medium seeks to allure, if not impose upon, the shallow-minded congregants. At no moment could the beneficial effects of these directions be more apparent than at the present epoch, when ritualism is rampant, and fine attire, parade and change in forms of garments seem no less attractive than Divine worship itself. Were there one specified attire for clergymen of all denominations, as was the case in the Jewish Temple, much acrimony would be avoided, and all dissent on that score hushed to rest.

The law which we are now about to consider is clearly intended to prevent a great social evil, which is only too intimately associated with immorality, if not with positive crime. It is to be found in Deut. ch. 22, v. v.—"The woman shall not wear that which pertaineth unto a man, neither shall a man put on a woman's garment, for all that do so are abomination unto the Lord." Assuredly God's commands may not be infringed with impunity, and those persons who disregard the injunction which forbids the wearing of an apparel appropriated to a different sex, as is only too frequently the practice in travesties during the Carnival, in the casinos in foreign lands, and even in fancy dress balls in our own country, oftentimes pay a heavy penalty and certainly incur the risk of obloquy and shame.

To show how admirably adapted to every situation and relation of life are even the least important of the Mosaic laws, and how beneficent are their intent, we would quote from Deut. ch. 24, v. v.—"When a man hath taken a new wife, he shall not go out to war, but he shall be free at home one year and shall cheer up his wife which he hath taken," for here we see that even a call to arms must not be suffered to destroy domestic happiness. Many, many a youthful widow in latter ages must have bemoaned the abandonment of an usage which had been directly commanded from on High.

Having now briefly passed in review some of the most important precepts found in the Pentateuch, it only remains to show how they may be most surely carried into practice, and how the injunction in Deut. ch. 19, *v.* iv., "Ye shall walk after the Lord thy God and keep his ordinances and fear Him, and serve Him," can be most easily made the rule of life. And assuredly these propositions may be concisely answered in the words of one command, truly the culminating point of Judaism—Deut. ch. 6, *v.* v.—"Thou shalt love the Lord with all thy heart," for then shall we with all our "soul and might" seek to fulfil each Divine behest, and thus make ourselves worthy of the love of Him who graciously gave us His Holy law "for our good always."

Before closing this chapter, it may fairly be asked if it is possible for the human mind to conceive that aught conducive to the well-being of man is lacking in that imperishable, that sublime code of the Israelite which we have had under consideration. Are not benevolence, true philanthropy, meekness of temper, forbearance, honesty, and every exalted virtue clearly enjoined therein, while is not every defect of character, every crime and all that would tend to vice and profligacy fully and clearly reprehended and forbidden? Embracing all that constitutes morality and true piety, the Mosaic Code needed indeed but God's seal to establish and confirm its perfection, which He, in His Supreme love towards His fallible creatures, graciously bestowed in the following explicit declaration—Deut. ch. 30, *v.* xx.—" For it (the law) is thy very life."

Chapter III.

Passing onwards from those laws which are pre-eminently distinguished for their sublime morality and practical utility, we will now give our attention to others which *seem* less perfect, and to which exception has been taken on the score that though they might have been of service at the time of their promulgation, and possibly were well-suited for a people just released from bondage, they are ill-adapted to promote the welfare of a civilized community at the present day! But is this really so? Assuredly not. If indeed the Mosaic Code of laws had emanated from fallible man, then we might readily believe that some imperfections would be discoverable therein, and that, like most human institutions, it could simply subserve a useful purpose in regard to some especial community or nation, and this for a limited time only. But when it is considered that each law, each injunction was given direct from Heaven, must not that man be presumptuous indeed, or wilfully blind, who dares question either their utility or practicability, who will set bounds to their duration or hold in low estimation any one ordinance, any one command which has proceeded from Omniscience? Yet there are to be found very many cavillers, who unhesitatingly aver that some of those laws of Divine origin are not only Draconic, but moreover are tyrannical and of cruel intent!

To disprove such erroneous and rash assertions will now be our aim, and we hope forthwith to show that even those few laws which appear to admit of a less satisfactory interpretation than the others, still bear the stamp of excellence, and that they only need a thoughtful and unprejudiced consideration to draw us to this conclusion.

Referring firstly to the several statutes in the Mosaic Code that relate to the punishment of death for certain grave offences and crimes, and which have been most unjustly designated harsh and vindictive by many men of unreflecting or prejudiced minds, it will simply be necessary to disprove such unfounded allegations by the plainest facts drawn from the records of History. These, indeed, do far more, since clearly testifying to the benefits which they conferred by promoting individual happiness, social well-being and public morality. And once again we would repeat that the certain knowledge that those laws directly emanated from the One Sole Fount of infinite love and perfection, should of itself suffice to enforce the conviction that they contain the germs of good to human kind, and assuredly none but the narrow and shallow-minded, who would dwarf all to the standard of their own defective or distorted vision, can fail to discern that they are characterized by wisdom, mercy and justice.

Now be it observed in the first place that the crimes to which are attached the penalty of death, were those that had been solemnly denounced from Sinai, and if suffered to be perpetrated with impunity, great demoralization must have infallibly followed, involving a serious disorganization in the entire community. We may instance the case of an undutiful and obdurate son, who, dead to filial affection and regardless of the Fifth Commandment and the voice of conscience, would surely have lost every spark of goodness by the time of reaching manhood but for the stern, yet salutary, punishment which might be lawfully enforced to arrest him in his wilful course. We may reasonably infer that fear of a violent and ignominious death proved an efficient deterrent, since we find no one instance in the pages of either sacred or profane Jewish History of a son having forfeited his life through running counter to the will of his parent. Here, then, we have ample ground for believing that to the very stringency of the command at Deut. ch. 21, v. xxi., "All the men of his city shall stone him with stones, that he die; so shalt thou put evil away from among you, and all Israel shall hear and fear," was due the fact of its never having been carried out in practice, and therefore it must have been, like every one of God's laws, all powerful for good. But the very manner of the threatened death, as well as the circumstances under which it had to be put in execution, was of itself well calculated to cure even the most heartless and rebellious youth. It would further have served as an example and a warning, since it was at the hands of the people that the penalty of the law was to be carried out, thus enabling them publicly to manifest their utter abhorrence of all insubordination to parental authority.

The infraction of the sixth commandment, "Thou shalt not kill," was also punishable with death, as we read in Num. ch. 35, *v.* xvi., "And if he smite him with an instrument of iron, or with throwing a stone so that he die, he is a murderer; the murderer shall surely be put to death." Again, in Lev. ch. 24, *v.* xvii., "And he that killeth any man shall surely be put to death." Human life was to be held sacred, and no one dare, under any possible circumstance, take the law into his own hands, or could with impunity seek to deprive a fellow-creature of this heavenly-bestowed gift. Thence Biblical history makes no mention of duelling, which till lately was so rife in many a civilised country, and unhappily is not even yet extinct. The code of honour instituted by man and instigated by a false sensibility could not exist simultaneously with the Divine law, which was clearly prohibitory of duelling, since its enforcement ensured the death of the victor following close on that of his victim. Surely no human being who appreciates the gift of life, and considers it criminal to stain the hand with the blood of a fellow-mortal, can deem that law too harsh or severe which restrains the man who, in his blind infatuation, would rashly and culpably take what no earthly power can restore, thereby committing a crime that no after repentance can efface or annul.

Now when we consider next the painful, heartless cases which even in the present day are frequently brought before the Divorce Court, it might well be asked, would such things be, if the seventh commandment was laid to heart, and the following injunctions of the same character, to be found in Num. ch. 5, *v*. xv. to xxiv., and in Lev. ch. 18, *v*. xx., were yet held in full force? Death for the breach of conjugal fidelity solemnly promised in the face of Heaven may seem a severe punishment, but if it is calculated to uphold public morality, to save many a household from a load of misery and shame, and keep would-be criminal stragglers in the path of virtue, surely it fulfils its wise intent, its highly moral purpose. And here again the beneficial result is practically manifested in the fact that the pages of Jewish history, comprising the annals of long centuries, have no such blot on record, except, alas! the one instance only too memorable in the Sacred Volume.

The penalty of death was likewise attached to the desecration of the Sabbath, which was a flagrant sin, since it involved disobedience to the will of God, as expressly set forth in the Decalogue, and he who would be capable of wilfully acting in opposition to one command of the Supreme, would surely depart from the straight line of duty on the slightest provocation, and violate other laws which were graciously given by Omniscience for the benefit of all mankind.

Witchcraft, to which the spiritualism of the present day bears only too close an affinity, was, like idolatrous worship, punishable with death, which of itself plainly shows that in the sight of heaven it was a gross abuse of man's free will, and, if left unchecked, would most certainly lead to every species of superstition with many an attendant evil. Here, again, there is nothing to warrant the belief that capital punishment for the infraction of the salutary laws prohibitory of witchcraft and idolatry was ever resorted to, indeed, all historical data lead to the very reverse inference, since hardly a single instance of condemnation for any one of the above-mentioned offences and crimes is to be found in the records of the Civil Court of Judea, whilst it is clearly stated by trustworthy writers that THAT Sanhedrim was deemed sanguinary which passed the sentence of death once in seventy years! Does not this fact of itself demonstrate how ripe with good fruits were the Mosaic laws, which, if theoretically severe, were certainly far otherwise in practice? That they secured the desired effect of staying the wilful, the weak-minded, the presumptous in their rash and evil course can admit of no reasonable doubt, and this was surely due in no small degree to the fear of a terrible retribution. Thus by a strict adherence to the Mosaic laws all mal-practices, all debauch, violence and crime were arrested, if not altogether extinguished in that nation which was commanded " to be holy, because the Lord thy God is holy."

But other causes were also at work to make the punishment of death a rare occurrence in Judea, and to these it may be well to refer before dismissing this subject, since they will serve to prove not only that leniency has ever been a high and notable characteristic of the Mosaic dispensation, but was likewise a distinguishing trait in the legislation of the Israelites of old. And to set these forth with lucidity and exactness, it will simply be necessary to give some few extracts from a work called the "Hebrew Review,"* edited by T. Theodores; they are to be found in an article entitled "Administration of Justice among the Jews," in which are embodied many important statements and historical facts well worthy of perusal, as may be judged by the following brief quotations :—" Every part of judicial procedure in the Mosaic law is founded on these three principles—publicity of trials, liberty of defence for the accused, security against false testimony. Hence a single witness counts as nothing, two or three at least are necessary to establish evidence. The witness on whose declaration a citizen is to be arraigned must previously be conducted before the priests and judges, and there take a solemn oath in the name of the Eternal, that his statement is the truth. The trial is to be held before every member of the community, whence false testimony is at every instant in danger of being brought to light by some one of the surrounding

---

* Vol. 3, page 8.

"persons. Finally, after sentence has been passed, the leading witness is the first whose hand hurls the deadly stone against the condemned brother, &c. It was of signal advantage to the culprit that he had the faculty of being tried at his choice, either by the council of his own city, by the minor council of Jerusalem, or by the high Sanhedrim. By these means he was protected against the fatal influence which local prejudices might, in many cases, engender. Great was the fear lest aught but the purest motives of equity and love of justice, could guide the judge who stood on any point of intimacy, or was at variance with the contending parties, or the person charged with an offence, and hence the extensive latitude left to the prisoner in the choice and rejection of the arbiters of his destiny." Again (at page 22), "The depositions of the witnesses were taken with the greatest circumspection, and the least discrepancy in their details obtained a verdict of acquittal for the prisoner. During the sitting of the court the auditors present were at liberty to ascend the judgment seat, and to employ all their eloquence, if they intended to speak in favour of the delinquent.

"No such right was granted them if condemnation was the motive of their application. At any stage of the proceedings the prisoner was at liberty to interrupt the debates and to call upon the assembly to listen to his defence, and he was ever allowed the benefit of a scruple, where a point of law rendered the decision difficult. If the majority of opinion was favourable to the prisoner, he was immediately set at liberty; but if the majority of elders had found him guilty, the court adjourned till the third day, when the magistrates again repaired to the seat of justice, and those who had found no reason to retract their verdict, showed their adhesion to the same by a repetition of their sentence. But as a generous trait in Hebrew legislation, it may be remarked that only those elders who had found a verdict of guilty on the day of the trial could change their sentence into an acquittal. The word of mercy once pronounced could no more be revoked. Of the twenty-three votes, twelve favourable ones were sufficient for the liberation of the accused, whereas it required more than twelve on the side of the prosecution to elicit a sentence of guilty. And even after the sentence of death "was pronounced, every precaution was taken to allow the prisoner a chance to retrieve his forfeited life, in case his innocence should come to light at that late hour. On the prisoner's own request, if he had any disclosures to make, he was taken back before the court as often as five times. Only when every chance of reprieve was impossible, the sentence of death was passed, and at a short distance from the place of punishment a soporific was administered to him, which had the effect of making him less sensible of the horrors of death." . . . Surely after perusing such testimony, founded as it is on indisputable data and authority, none but the most sceptical will be disposed to dispute our statement that the Jewish Tribunals left naught undone which could hedge round human life, although due punishment was administered in conformity with a strict sense of justice and God's all-gracious laws.

And now we may proceed to consider the oft quoted sentence, Ex. ch. 21, v. xxiv., which alludes to the brutal assaulter of the weaker sex, and is repeated in almost identical terms in reference to the "false witness," at Deut. ch. 19, v. xxi., "Life shall go for life,* eye for eye, tooth for tooth," &c., which, despite the whole scope and teachings of Mosaism, has only too frequently been strangely, grossly misconceived and unfairly interpreted. The idea that this injunction inculcates a spirit of retaliation, that it breathes a feeling of revenge which can alone be appeased by returning evil for evil, displays such an utter lack of discernment that assuredly it could only be entertained either by a novice unversed in Sacred history, or by a mind blinded by prejudice and infatuation. Truly all scriptural evidence runs directly counter to such a supposition, and surely any-

* Let those who cavil at this Mosiac command, and can so far misinterpret its practical bearings as to declare it harsh and vindictive, take cognizance of these memorable words, uttered by the highest legal authority in the most civilised Christian country in Europe. The Lord Chief Justice, after having passed sentence of death on a murderer (see Criminal Court in the *Times* of the 2nd of December, 1875) thus addressed the culprit; " I have to warn you against any delusive hope of mercy here as long as *the law exists which says that he who takes the life of a fellow-creature with malice aforethought shall answer for it with his own.*" Surely then we have here sufficient evidence to convince the most sceptical that the Divine injunction was not given merely to suit the exigences of the time of its promulgation, but was adapted to secure the cause of order and the well-being of humanity in after ages by the strict enforcement of justice and equity, which must and ever will prove the surest, the most efficacious deterrant to all violence and crime.

one who has seriously considered the imperative injunction, "thou shalt not avenge," could not for one moment imagine any law, however seemingly harsh and exceptionally severe, to be so in reality, since it would fail to correspond, not only with the all-important command "thou shalt love thy neighbour as thyself," which ordinance is the only true standard whereby Judaism should be judged, but also with very many more of the like humane and merciful statutes which have been treated on at some length in the previous chapter.

But granting that we take the command "eye for eye, foot for foot, &c.," in its harshest sense, it would yet be easy to show that it was in itself a merciful and wise ordinance, calculated to proportion the punishment to the crime, scare the *wilful* evil-doer, and curb the irascible, vindictive, remorseless man through the dread of undergoing a similar fate. It served as a powerful restraint, and one only too greatly needed in a clime where the passions of men were oftentimes apt to become ungovernable. And surely it must be conceded by those who have attentively studied the history of the middle ages that had this law then been in force, its pages would not be sullied by so many a sickening list of horrors and tragical deeds entailing intense human suffering and misery; truly, many an act of violence and crime would never have been perpetrated had the penalty for the evil inflicted been precisely commensurate to the wrong done. And further, admitting that the imposition of severe retribution was to be literally interpreted, yet it should be taken in connection with the attendant circumstances and especially with the method in which it was carried out. The cause was brought before the highest tribunal of the land and was adjudged by those elders who had the full confidence of the entire nation. The adjustment of all criminal proceedings depended entirely on the fiat of the judges, as commanded in Ex. ch. 21, v. xxii., and Deut. ch. 19, v. xviii. Also be it remembered that it was with the most scrupulous nicety that these elected judges examined and investigated every act, sifting all the evidence that could be procured before delivering the final sentence, whilst under no possible circumstance could a penalty be imposed without at least two witnesses testifying on oath to the alleged deed, and swearing in open court to a positive knowledge of the crime imputed to the accused. The accuser was bound publicly to prove that he had dealt fairly, and the more surely to secure truthful testimony, the false witness had to undergo a fearful retribution, inasmuch as the award which he would have brought on another was decreed against himself, for we read in Deut. ch. 19, v. xvi., "If a false witness rise up against any man to testify against him that which is wrong;" v. xix., "then shall ye do unto him as he had thought to have done unto his brother; so shall ye put evil away from among you." Assuredly we have in these facts enough to prove to demonstration that the command, so inconsiderately, so unjustly criticised, was truly in direct antagonism to a spirit of vindictiveness; that the wilful murderer and the obdurate defier of God's gracious laws would surely meet an ignominious fate at the hand of justice, must necessarily have precluded a recourse to individual or private revenge.

Here we may also remark that could it be certified in any case that accident and not premeditated ill-will was the cause of injury or death to a fellow-mortal, then was the city of refuge open to the unhappy author of the deed. [Deut. ch. 4, *v.* xli.] Thus it will be seen that none but the wilful offender or murderer need stand in dread of retributive justice. And to prove the leniency which ever characterizes the Jewish law, we must further note that any such penalty lasted only for a time, since on the death of the High Priest the exile might return to his own home free from all fear of incurring any hostility or personal inconvenience. Nor should we ignore the fact that a sentence being once passed acquitting a prisoner, no further proceedings with regard to the same offence could be instituted. Now before concluding this subject, once again must we repeat that history fails to point to one single instance of the execution of the law " eye for eye, tooth for tooth," thereby showing most conclusively, that either this injunction was not literally interpreted by the Sanhedrim, or that if indeed it were considered of practical application, then it had efficiently served the beneficial purpose for which it was instituted, and must have saved many a man from perpetrating deeds of violence and crime.

And be it observed that the law of restitution

to be found embodied and detailed in Ex. ch. 22, v. i. to xv., was very similar in character and effect. The mere dread that a penalty would be imposed assimilating to the fraud committed, tended to keep in check the avaricious and crafty man, the imposter, and the thief. Additional evidence might easily be adduced to substantiate the foregoing facts, but further remarks on this score seem superfluous; thence we will now revert to another Jewish law which affords one more proof that leniency, and certainly not harshness, was the prominent feature of the Mosaic code. We read in Deut. ch. 25, v. iii., "If the wicked man be worthy to be beaten, forty stripes may be given *and not exceed*, lest if he should exceed and beat him above these, then thy brother should seem vile unto thee." Now surely it is impossible to reconcile this injunction with the belief that the Jewish creed ever permitted, much less demanded, rigorous measures and inculcated the sacrifice of mercy to justice, and if thus much be granted, what then becomes of all unfavourable strictures on this score. No, here again the heavenly-bestowed law is not at fault, but rather those, who through gross ignorance or malice-propense, have dared to take exception to it. Man would be wiser than his Maker!

It will now be necessary to revert briefly to the subject of Usury, a word which, as clearly shown in the previous chapter, was used in the place of "interest," a very important difference truly, since its supposed practice has often been regarded as a blot in the character of the Judaic race. Now there could hardly be any more erroneous belief than that the Mosaic Code counselled usury in the case of the alien, and we would quote from the writings of an able scholar, the Rev. Dr. H. Adler, in testimony of the application of a far more beneficent law. Here are his words:—"When the Gentile needed the loan of money, not for commerce but for his subsistence, our Divine law made no difference between him and the Hebrew." We read in Lev. ch. 25, v. xxxv., xxxvi., "And if thy brother be waxen poor, then thou shalt relieve him; yea, *though he be a stranger or sojourner*, that he may live with thee. *Take no usury of him or increates*, but fear the Lord." Could any injunction be more equitable, more just? yet has it been ungenerously and unfairly asserted that the prohibition to lend at an usurious rate did not extend to the alien, but simply to a brother in faith. Accept the correct word, "interest" in lieu of usury, mark the repeated inculcation of justice and charity towards the stranger, and further, bear in mind that the practice of usury in its true sense was even punishable with death, see Ezek. ch. 18, v. xiii., "He that hath given forth upon usury, *and hath taken increase:* shall he then live? he shall not live; he hath done *this abomination,* he shall surely die; his blood shall be upon him;" and then declare whether it is not utterly erroneous to say that the Jewish law inculcated usurious dealings; and, indeed, had there been no other command than the one in Lev. ch 25, v. xiv., "Ye shall not oppress one another," it would amply suffice to disprove any such assertion.

But among the numerous ordinances which tended to discourage covetousness and greediness of gain, there were none more efficacious than, firstly, the observance of the Sabbath when all trafficking was to be suspended; secondly, the jubilee, or year of release, during which the restoration of all property and personal freedom was ordained; thirdly, the festivals, when gifts were to be liberally made to the needy; and lastly, the sacrifices, which demanded and enforced freewill offerings for the benefit of the Levite, the widow, and the orphan.

And it is this latter subject that now calls for our attention, since the end and aim of the Sacrificial ordinances being frequently misunderstood, and their wise and beneficent intent inadvertently ignored or carelessly disregarded, many have been led to cavil at and adversely criticise this phase of Temple worship. It will not, however, be necessary to dwell on more than the main point, for, like several Levitical and economical precepts and practices, the commands relating to sacrifice were solely to be held in force by the Hebrew people *during their sojourn in Judea*. Truly, great was the good the sacrificial offerings at that period conferred: they gave a vent for gratitude and thankfulness to God in a practical shape; they served as a token of truthful repentance; they proved an admirable medium for dispensing charity, the rich, in accordance with God's solemn command, being bound to offer up *the best* of their flocks and herds, while the priest and the needy were thereby assured of ample provision in the shape of wholesome animal food. Not the most avaricious and grasping man dared appear empty before the Lord: he was forced to do his duty towards the poor as well as towards his Maker, even if too callous to fulfil voluntarily the imperative obligation which the wealthy owe to the indigent and destitute. That the sacrifices were the means to an end, and not the end itself, admits of no reasonable doubt; indeed, no small proportion of them were left to the promptings of the natural and pious feelings of the Israelitish people. In conclusion, it is enough to remark that as Abel, Noah, and the patriarchs offered up of their own free will a "sweet savour to the Lord" to evince their grateful remembrance of some especial manifestation of Divine goodness and bounty, so did the sacrifices in the Temple admit of the pious worshipper showing a practical acknowledgment of his undying belief in God's beneficence, mercy, and loving kindness. Who, then, dare affirm that they were objectless, fruitless, or superfluous?

We may now say a few words on the various commands relative to slavery which are embodied in the Mosaic dispensation, and surely it will only need some careful reflection on their purport to arrive at the firm conviction that, although forming an element in the social conditions of Judea, it nevertheless left no dark stain whatsoever on the heavenly-inspired Code, as has so often been inconsiderately affirmed. First, however, be it remembered that slavery, like polygamy, was simply tolerated, and most certainly never enjoined; indeed, there is every reason to believe that it was permitted in consideration of the peculiar position held by the Israelites in regard to the surrounding idolatrous nations, and which made it almost imperative to hold as bondsmen those prisoners taken by them in war, whilst it must surely have been in a great measure the fear of servitude attending on capture and defeat, which curbed these warlike and barbarous tribes. And of this we may adduce a proof from the Book of Joshua, where we find in chapter 9 that the Gibeonites yielded *of themselves* submissively to become "hewers of wood and drawers of water," and said to the Jewish Leader—" Now, behold, we are in thy hand; as it seemeth good and right unto thee to do unto us, do." The better to show that slavery was only tolerated, and that few were subjected to it except prisoners of war, we have but to refer to Ex. ch. 21, v. xvi., "He that stealeth a man and selleth him, or if he be found in his hand, he shall surely be put to death;" for here we have distinct proof that all trafficking in human beings and servitude through surreptitious means were not only against the Mosaic Code, but even entailed the penalty of death. It should, however, be borne in mind that the condition of the slave under the Jewish dispensation was totally unlike the serfdom of which we read in profane history; truly it was only the mildest form of thraldom, and there being but "one manner of law for the stranger and for one of the land," it is clear that the numerous injunctions which prohibited unkindness and severity to the needy brother who had sold himself into servitude was equally applicable to the alien slave. But had there been no other law than that to be found in Ex. ch. 21, v. xxvi., "If a man smite the eye of his servant that it perish, he shall let him go free for his eye's sake; if he smite out his tooth, he shall let him go free for his tooth's sake;" this would suffice to prove that the bond slave had no cause to fear mal-treatment, for a blow struck or such violence used as would maim him, was adequate to procure his liberation, a pecuniary penalty which no master would voluntarily incur or dare ignore. If, then, it could be said that there was any harshness in this case, it certainly was against the oppressor and in favour of the oppressed and humble slave. Yet additional evidence that slavery was no Mosaic institution, but merely the result of the necessity which existed for it during the earlier organisation of the nation, is to be found in the fact that for the building of the Temple levies were raised among the Israelites themselves, and that to the number of thirty thousand; while the Syrians, who had been taken prisoners by King David, merely became his "servants;" indeed, only once in the history of the reign of Solomon do we find any mention of bondsmen, while a noted event narrated in the Book of Kings makes it clear that it was not the practice of that period to retain prisoners of war as slaves; else should we not read, that when King Jehoram asked Elisha, the prophet, what was to be done with the captive Syrians, he thus advised his monarch, " Set bread and water before them, so that they may go to their master," and this kindly act performed, "*he sent them away*" to their own land.

It would be a serious omission to conclude this especial chapter without making some reference to the numerous wars which the Israelites of old waged against their idolatrous neighbours, if only for the purpose of showing that far from having their origin in the teachings of Moses, or through the proclivities of the Hebrew people themselves, as has been affirmed by superficial readers of the Sacred volume, they simply arose from circumstances over which the nation could have no possible control. And first, be it observed, in refutation to much unmerited censure on this score, that no one instance of useless bloodshed is on record. When it was a direct command from God to exterminate an idolatrous nation which was immersed in crime and debauch, and dead to all feeling of remorse or repentance, or, when in the words of Scripture, " the iniquity of the Amonites was full," surely the Israelites must have felt it their bounden duty to obey the

Divine Behest, and therefore the individuals who impute blame to those who were simply the instruments chosen by the Lord Himself to fulfil His purpose, may not feel that they are altogether free from the presumptuous act of judging the gracious Ruler of the Universe, the great Judge of all. Surely it is sufficient to read (Ex. ch. 23, *v.* xxviii.), " I, the Lord, do drive them out," and (Deut. ch. 20, *v.* xvii.), " I will deliver the inhabitants of the land into thy hands"; and again, (Num. ch. 25, *v.* xvii.) " Vex the Midianites and *smite them*, for they vex you with their wiles," to be convinced that the Iraelites only resorted to arms against neighbouring states in obedience to the word of the Supreme, who, in His wisdom must have seen that to permit the further growth of idolatry, with its revolting practices, and the violation of every principle of right and humanity, might finally taint the beautiful world He had made, and entail unutterable misery and calamity on His creatures. God would not withdraw the gracious boon of freewill which might, according if wisely used or grossly abused, be made a blessing or a curse ; better that the impenitent sinner should pay the just penalty of his misdeeds, and therefore, assuredly, was the minor calamity of war permitted for the purpose of arresting the far greater and ever growing evil, the contaminating influence engendered by idolatry and superstition.

But while these wars were Divinely ordained, mark how they were to be conducted. On besieging a city, the first act required in accordance with the command to be found in Deut. ch. 23. v. x., was to "proclaim peace unto it." Surely, such an injunction proves beyond all doubt, that for the purpose of preventing any spirit of vindictiveness or revenge predominating, and thereby provoking a sanguinary conflict, such conflict had to be preceded by friendly overtures, which precluded the possibility of that reckless haste so frequently attending on violence, passion, and strife, while giving scope for mature deliberation, a wise circumspection, and above all, for a thoughtful consideration of what is due to our common humanity.

Surely, enough has now been advanced to show that nothing but love, clemency, and benevolence were inculcated in the Mosaic Code; and further, that these characteristics were displayed by the Israelites of old under almost every circumstance and condition, whilst even the stain that slavery and war seems to cast on the pages of their history, vanishes away on close investigation; thence, if any doubts could yet arise in regard to that mercy, that justice, which assuredly permeates the Jewish Code, they should be at once dismissed, and the conviction fostered, that God's laws are replete with all that can prove beneficial to His creatures; in a word, that they are wise, true, and perfect.

Chapter IV.

To the certain knowledge of the writer of these pages, many of the most enlightened Christians, and among them clergymen and dignitaries of the Church, entertain the erroneous conviction, surprisingly enough, that the Jews do not authoritatively believe in the immortality of the soul, and that it is not to the Old, but to the New Testament alone that mankind must turn to find this doctrine inferred and expounded.

Now, could this view be substantiated, and so all important, all vital an article of belief, be proved to have no place in Jewish ethics, then indeed would Mosaism have one vulnerable point of attack, but assuredly any such assertion is altogether ill founded, as we hope hereby to demonstrate.

Treating, as we are, on all the salient characteristics of Judaism, with its doctrinal excellences, it would be impossible to ignore this bulwark of Mosaism, thence the author here reproduces from his last religious work ("Moral Biblical Gleanings") a letter he addressed some years back to a dear relative on the subject of Immortality, and which, greatly to the satisfaction of the writer, has not only left a favourable impression on the minds of various readers, but has even led some of the thoughtful and enquiringly disposed of another creed to the conviction of the truths therein advanced, and to the knowledge that Judaism lacks no vital principle of stability, no doctrine that could possibly serve to promote man's well-being here or hereafter.

LETTER ON IMMORTALITY.

"Dear ——,—In fulfilment of my promise, I gladly place before you some of the numerous Biblical quotations which refer to the all-important subject of immortality. They are culled from the various Books of the Old Testament, and directly or indirectly bear testimony that belief therein has ever been the very essence of the Jewish faith.

"Referring, firstly, to the FIVE BOOKS OF MOSES, we find that almost all relating to a future state is of a *practical* character, thus *the death of the righteous Abel* by the hand of his "guilty brother, when considered in connection with the goodness of the Deity, affords ample evidence that this life is but the prelude to another and a better world. If death be annihilation, where was Abel's merited reward? God had no sooner testified His pleasure with the conduct of His pious servant, than death befel him! Surely, were there no future state, this untimely fate must be considered a chastisement, and certainly not a recompense for his past virtuous life, thence we *must* believe in immortality if we believe in the justice and goodness of God. The *death of Moses* speaks no less forcibly to the same effect. For one inconsiderate act he was not only denied the privilege of entering the Land of Promise, but had to yield up his life at the very moment that his hopes were about to meet their fruition! If dissolution of the mortal frame were indeed synonymous with extinction of the soul or spirit, breathed by God into man, we should assuredly be unable to reconcile the fact of his departure from this world at such a moment with the gracious attributes of the Lord. Truly the great law-giver, Moses, in his death added to his other valuable teachings the all-important "lesson that at the very gates of death lies life everlasting. The *translation of Enoch* to Heaven without dying is not without its significance; indeed, it goes far to prove that another habitation does exist for the sons of men, and is reserved for the faithful servants of the Lord.

"Other practical examples might be adduced, but we will now select some quotations from the same five Books, which are scarcely less conclusive. Take the sentence, Gen. ch. 15, *v*. xi., "Thou shalt *go to thy fathers* in peace;" also ch. 25, "He was *gathered unto his people;*" and what meaning may we attach to such words but the assurance of a future state? Indeed, when applied to Abraham, Moses, Aaron, Samuel, Jeremiah, and various others, it is evident that the *soul* and not the *body* is referred to, since not one of these was buried near his father, but *in distant sepulchres,* and in more than one instance, lonely solitudes, far, far from the haunts of men. These words would otherwise be worse than meaningless; they would not even bear the high stamp of truth, in itself an utter impossibility, proceeding as they did from the God of truth. Again, in Gen. ch. 47, we find Jacob alluding to the length of his *pilgrimage,* "and averring before Pharaoh that the years of his life had been "few and evil." Now the very word, pilgrimage, betokened his belief that this world was but a preparation for another, free from those trials which beset his path here on earth. Then among the divers laws given by Moses to the Israelites, we may note such expressions as these: Gen., "He who doeth this wrong *shall be utterly destroyed;*" "that *soul* shall be cut off," and again in Lev. "that *soul* shall be *utterly* cut off." Here death of the *soul* is threatened as a punishment, thereby clearly implying that a future world is reserved as a reward for the pious and virtuous. Then, what is more significant and expressive of the belief in immortality among the Israelites, than their impassioned words to Moses, Num. ch. 17, *v.* xii., "Behold, we die, we *perish,*" implying utter annihilation. Again, Moses thus addresses the people, Deut. 30, *v.* xix., "I call heaven and earth to record this day against you that I have set before you *life and death, therefore choose life,*" &c. Now, since death befals the virtuous no less than the evil-disposed and vicious, "life," evidently here implies life everlasting. Further, by the light of immor-

"tality alone could the people have understood the promised reward of Moses that "their days should be as the *days of heaven* upon the earth" would they but act in obedience to the Holy Law. And again, did not Moses clearly allude to a future life, when, after imploring forgiveness for his people, he added, "Yet now if Thou wilt not forgive their sin, then *blot me*, I pray Thee, *out of Thy Book*." Surely, such words must convince us that a belief in immortality, as well as future rewards and punishment, was entertained both by the lawgiver and his people.

"It is true, however, that the Five Books of Moses speak less plainly and touch more lightly on this subject, this belief, than the Psalms or the Prophets, but the reason is obvious; like prayer, it is an instinct, a craving of the human heart, and therefore, like it, was never especially "commanded." Further, Moses could not consistently set himself to impress a people, but lately emancipated from slavery, leading a wandering life and deeply engrossed in every-day cares, with the doctrine of prospective advantages in a future life, but this he knew full well, that when their minds "became enlightened they would not only comprehend, but would even grasp its full and high import. It sufficed that he had laid a foundation with ample materials to develop the superstructure into a fundamental principle in future generations. And as we pass onwards, reviewing the various portions of Scripture, this truth openly reveals itself. We find that when once the Israelites had freed themselves from their enemies and established a powerful Kingdom, then, and then only, were they enabled to dismiss the overwhelming cares of the moment, and turn their thoughts into loftier channels. Spiritual welfare was then considered as well as the well-being of the body. Of this we may feel convinced when we peruse the beautiful *Psalms of David*, which repeatedly revert to the immortality of the soul. These were written *for the entire people*, and had they not already entertained a well-grounded hope of a blessed hereafter, David's allusions thereto would have been totally unintelligible to them. How could they have comprehended such passages as these, Ps. 23, v. iii., "The Lord *restoreth my soul;*" Ps. 119, v. xv., "God will *redeem my soul from the power of the grave*, he will "receive me," and Ps. 97, *v.* x., "Ye that love the Lord hate evil, He *preserveth the soul of His saints;*" and again Ps. 37, *v.* xxxvii., "Mark the perfect man, for the end of that man is *peace;*" such peace being the sure result of a firm belief in life eternal, for holy trust ever banishes all fear, all doubts, all questionings. Then we have David's memorable words addressed to his *servants* on the death of his son; "While the child lived, I fasted and prayed, for who could tell whether God will be gracious to me that it may live, but now that he is dead, wherefore should I fast? can I bring him back again? *I shall go to him*, but he will not return to me." Surely this answer alone would afford conclusive evidence of his faith in a world beyond the grave. Again, how may we construe the following words of Abigail to David, if not persuaded that they allude to immortality? I. Samuel ch. 25, "The *soul* of my Lord shall be bound in the bundle of life with the Lord thy God," thence showing that the belief not only animated the King, but had taken a firm hold on the mind of the whole people. Although more wordly-minded, Solomon spoke no less forcibly or distinctly of a future "state than did his father David. His words are not to be misunderstood, being entirely free from all ambiguity. Thus in Eccles. we read, "All go to one place, all are of the dust, and all turn to dust again; who knoweth *the spirit of man that goeth upwards?*" and ch. 12, "Man goeth to his long home; then shall the dust return to the earth as it was, and *the spirit will return unto God who gave it.*" Then in Proverbs, which were especially adapted for the people, we read, ch. 11, "Righteousness *delivereth from death;*" also, we are told, "When the wicked man *dieth, his expectation shall perish;*" and again, "In the way of righteousness is *life*, and in the pathway thereof *there is no death.*"

"We now turn to the *Book of Job*, supposed to have been written in the time of Moses; and therein we find additional proof that the blissful hope of immortality was *then* a belief, a fixed trust. Thus we read ch. 19 —" and after this *body is destroyed*, out of my flesh shall I see God." Again, " God looked upon men, and if any say, I have sinned, then *will He deliver his soul*, and *his life shall see the light.*"

"A few practical incidents calculated to strengthen the belief in immortality may be

" here introduced ; for example, when Elijah prayed to God that Zarephath's child's *soul* should come into him again, the Lord granted his request, and "*the soul came back unto him again,* and he revived." Then also the *translation of Elijah* himself clearly proves that there is another habitation for the sons of men.

" Turning next to the *Book of Kings,* we find that in more than one instance *death was promised as a blessing, as a reward for virtuous conduct,* as in the case of that excellent monarch Josiah, 2 Kings ch. 22, *v.* xx. ; yet could this have been deemed such by monarchs in the zenith of their prosperity, had they not firmly and fixedly believed in immortality?

"And now we may add some quotations from the Books of the *Prophets,* written at various epochs, most of them in the reigns of the Jewish Kings, but some few when a portion of the Israelites had become captives and exiles in the land of their enemies. Thus we read in Isaiah ch. 26, *v.* xix., " The *dead* shall *live. Awake* and sing, ye that dwell in dust," &c. Again, ch. 55, *v.* iii., " Incline your ear and come unto me, saith the Lord, and *your soul shall live.* Let the wicked man forsake his "way and turn unto the Lord, and God will *abundantly pardon.*" And again how significant is the following sentence, ch. 25, *v.* viii., "He, the Lord, *will swallow up death in victory.*" Next, extracting from *Jeremiah*, ch. 22 *v.* x., "Weep ye not for the dead, neither bemoan him, but weep sore for him that goeth away (into exile) *for* HE *shall return no more.*" Then what words could be more significant of eternal life than the following of Ezekiel ch. 13, *v.* xix., "Thus said the Lord God, will ye pollute me among my people *to slay the souls that should not die?*" Again, speaking of a righteous man, ch. 18, *v.* ix., "He hath walked in my statutes, and hath kept my judgments to deal truly, *he is just, he shall surely live*, saith the Lord." Also, alluding to the evil-doer, "When the wicked man turneth away from his wickedness that he hath committed, and doeth that which is lawful and right, *he shall save his soul alive;*" and again, ch. 33, *v.* xv., "If the wicked restore the pledge, &c., *walk in the statutes of life*, without committing iniquity, *he shall surely live, he shall not die.*"

"Turning next to *Daniel*, we read ch. 12— "And at that time thy people shall be delivered, "*every one that shall be found written in the Book*, and many of them that sleep in the dust shall awake, *some to everlasting life*, &c., and they that be wise shall shine as the brightness of the firmament, and they that turn many to righteousness *as the stars for ever and ever.*' Then in Hosea ch. 13, *v.* ix., "O, Israel, thou hast *destroyed thyself*, but in Me is thine help; *I will ranson them from the power of the grave*, I will *redeem them from death*." Lastly, in Malachi ch. 3, "They that feared the Lord *spake often one to another*, and the Lord hearkened, and a *Book of remembrance was written before him* for them that feared the Lord and that thought upon his name." Truly, a reiteration of the words of Moses, containing the same glorious promise to the good and righteous.

"PROFANE HISTORY further yields ample evidence that the Biblical teachings of immortality were not lost upon the Jewish nation. During long years thousands died for their religion, and by their willing martyrdom not only proved their love and trust in the One sole God, but also practically demonstrated their belief in a future and happier state. To those who thus perished, "death was not annihilation, but an entrance into realms of bliss. The *writings of the learned Israelites* of successive generations give additional testimony that this belief has never been extinct in the nation. And finally, as a conclusive proof that the immortality of the soul is, and ever was, an essential *principle* among the Jews, we need only turn to the *thirteen fundamental articles* of their faith wherein this belief is clearly embodied. Now, had not Moses in his five Books inculcated this doctrine, had it been a mere instinct or the offshoot of another creed, this tenet could not possibly have found a place there. Assuredly, that which Moses taught or commanded, and *nothing else*, forms the basis of the Jewish Faith. To his teachings, then, is this belief due, and if it has in a measure grown and strengthened in successive generations, such is but the natural consequence of the increase of enlightenment, and the ever-growing supremacy of reason and Faith."

Chapter V.

Having passed in review several important enactments and tenets embodied in the belief of the pious Israelite, and given especial attention to those laws and statutes which are the very basis of the Mosaic religion and have remained intact during ages of tribulation and persecution, it may now be well to consider the beneficial and highly moral influence these latter have exercised on the Jewish nation ever since their promulgation, and as this can best be accomplished by the light of biography, we will summon a host of Jewish celebrities whose united examples cannot fail to prove a tower of strength, since each one has clearly demonstrated through his individual life, that those laws have sufficed to form a truly moral, virtuous, exalted character, and have further conduced to develop the highest intellectual powers.

Referring, firstly, to Biblical History, it is easy to perceive what a beneficial influence the

Mosaic Code exercised at all those periods when the Israelites followed the prescribed ordinances, and possibly this was never more marked than during the first half century after the Exodus from Egypt. The following words of Joshua—"Ye have kept all that Moses, the servant of the Lord, commanded you. . . . Cleave unto the Lord your God, as ye have done unto this day," uttered only some forty years after the deliverance of the poor downtrodden slaves, would not fail to create surprise, if we could allow ourselves to believe that the moral improvement here notified in the character of the succeeding generation was due to any adventitious cause, ignoring the true one, viz.,—the strict observance of the sublime laws given direct from Heaven, which had been rigidly enjoined by its first recipients on their offspring. Then it is on record how high the nation rose some years later, when, after relapsing into idolatry, they once again sought their God, and followed His statutes as prescribed by Samuel; indeed, throughout the whole Biblical history, it is clearly discernible that they became the more prosperous and mighty in proportion as they observed God's wise and gracious ordinances. This is evident as we pass in review the reigns of David,* Solomon, Hezekiah, Josiah, at which times they reared their heads high, and made themselves respected or feared by every surrounding nation.

Further, if we merely glance over the names of some of the most distinguished Israelites of old, and mark their many estimable traits of character and their many virtues, we must arrive at the conclusion that it was simply necessary to follow implicitly the heavenly-given code in order to reach the highest moral excellence and take foremost rank among the best, the noblest, who have adorned the world's history. And here it may be mentioned it was with this object the author of these pages entered at some length on a biographical sketch of most of the scriptural characters in his work entitled "Moral Biblical Gleanings and *Practical Teachings;*" and as this book could be referred to, it will here suffice to bring into prominence

---

* It may be well to remark that the Exodus from Egypt was in 1490 B.C., while the reign of David began in 1060, for we may thus perceive that it only required 430 years to effect a most marvellous transformation, the Israelitish nation being at the very zenith of its power and grandeur at the later date.

a *few* of those faithful servants of God who regulated their lives in accordance with His laws, and through some transcendent virtue, or some memorable deed, have bequeathed an invaluable lesson to posterity and left behind them an imperishable name. Could we possibly begin with a better example than that of the Great Lawgiver himself—MOSES, the meekest of men? Did he not by his self-abnegation, his forbearance under the severest provocation, expound the sublime precept (Lev. ch. 19, *v.* xviii.), "Thou shalt love thy neighbour as thyself"? a precept which takes precedence in moral ethics, and which was first promulgated by him who well knew how to practice what he taught. Take next the following lives, and surely we must acknowledge that in every instance the distinctive features of each character are based on principles derived from the Mosaic Code. In the dauntless *Joshua* we mark courage, disinterestedness, and a love of duty; in the zealous *Phinehas*, we find a proved champion of moral right; in the pious *Samuel*, a spotless integrity; in the God-fearing *David*, holy faith, earnestness in right doing and sincere repentance after transgression; in the Godly

Elijah, a bold reprover of kings and zealous servant of the Most High; in the true-hearted *Elisha*, a dutiful and loving son, a generous and forgiving spirit, one who counselled the free dismissal of captive foes and personal enemies after conferring benefits on 'them; in the prayful *Jeremiah*, a true patriot, undaunted by threats and piously submissive under trials and calamaties, bearing ill-deserved scorn and contumely with dignified magnanimity; in the humble *Mordecai*, we note a man who disdained to be a sycophant and bow to greatness; and again, in the "greatly beloved" *Daniel*, who in a land of idolatry remained faithful to his God and faced without dismay perils attendant on his conscientious allegiance to the Most High.

We will now pass from Biblical to profane History, and briefly sketch forth in chronological order such important events, with their consequent change in the condition of the nation, as owe their origin, either to a religious movement on the part of the entire Jewish people, or to the impulse given by some individual member thereof through his courage, learning, or religious zeal.

Commencing this necessarily condensed commentary at the period of the building of the second Temple, which was accomplished after some years, in spite of innumerable obstacles and various impediments placed in the way by both internal and external foes, we must remark that this great and glorious achievement was due chiefly to the fervour, courage and persistency of *Ezra*, combined with an energetic spirit on the part of the entire community worthy of the high intent. From the moment of its dedication, true piety predominated over idolatry, and the sabbaths and festivals were kept " with joy." Some twenty years later, Alexander the Great visited this Jewish Temple, and although he came as a foe, he nevertheless departed as a friend, owing to the respect with which the High Priest had inspired him. After this incident, not ten years elapsed before Judea became a prey to various rapacious and ambitious foreign Monarchs, who, with vast armies, over-ran and conquered the country, then depopulated it by carrying away with them hundreds of thousands of captives as slaves. This state of warfare lasted with little intermission some 180 years, when up rose the heroic family of the Maccabees, and through the valor and strategic ability of JUDAH MACCABEE, the Syrians were defeated with great slaughter.* When once peace was re-established, this chivalrous patriot caused the Temple to be purified and Divine worship restored, and during the six years that he administered the affairs of Judea, his merits, military, civil and religious, were gladly acknowledged by the whole population. Great indeed, were the services he rendered his country, for he had found it depopulated, the fields lying waste, commerce utterly paralyzed, and ruin general, whilst at his death agriculture was again progressing, commerce had completely revived, life and property were secure, and the land teeming with population; Judah Maccabees was, indeed, a true champion of Israel, and the revival of a devout spirit throughout the nation was greatly due to his

---

* And unequal indeed on one occasion was the contest, the Hebrew army consisting of only eight hundred men against thirty times that number of well-trained Syrian troops! Surely no such feat of arms is upon record, if we except the noted one of the three hundred Spartans at Thermopylæ. And, indeed, what but love of country and love of God could induce eight hundred men to face such fearful odds!

zeal and earnestness in the cause of religion. At his decease he was deeply and deservedly mourned by the entire community.

Twenty-six years later the Roman rule commenced, and many were the trials the Jews had to undergo during the supremacy of that nation, which, after lasting just one hundred and twenty years, culminated in a revolt of the whole Jewish population. This was especially fomented by the extreme cruelty of the Roman Governor, Florus, who executed many of the nobility, massacred some twenty thousand of the people, and sent large numbers to the galleys. To quell this insubordination, vast armies were poured into the country and fearful was the slaughter of the Israelites, forty thousand falling during the gallant defence of Jotapala. On one battle field alone thirty-six thousand were taken prisoners, then sold for slaves, and finally A.D. 68, Jerusalem was taken, and the Temple burnt to the ground.* We find here

---

* If it were needed to prove the steadfast devotion of the Jew to his country and his religion, it would be enough to state the fact that before Judea was finally subjugated, about one million and a half of this devoted people perished, only one hundred thousand submitting to their conquerors.

no cowardly submission, but rather a heroism which could only have derived its vigor from the purest patriotism and a fervor inspired by the holy, the sublime Mosaic religion.

It was just one hundred years after the death of Judah Maccabee, that the college of HILLEL flourished. And mark the favourite precepts which this truly pious and enlightened Israelite inculcated in his disciples, "Love peace and pursue it; *love mankind and cause them to approach the law;*" and "Let thy conduct towards *all men* be regulated by the dictates of mercy and justice." A worthy teacher truly! A few years later, during the reign of Adrian, the Jews had to bow before the most cruel prohibitions, indeed, they were not allowed to practice or observe their most sacred rites, instant death following upon any infringement of the King's commands, and it was at this season of severe trial that the custom was introduced of reading sections from the Prophets during divine service in lieu of portions of the law which had been arbitrarily interdicted. During this period of persecution and tribulation, flourished Rabbi AKIBA, who, after benefitting his co-religionists by his pious labours and "constructing a fence round the law," was put to a cruel death together with nine other sages of note. But better times were at hand, and this change was chiefly owing to Rabbi JUDAH, the Prince, who through his virtue, piety, and learning, obtained the esteem and respect of Antoninus Pius and three successive Emperors, during whose reigns the Jews enjoyed all the rights of their Roman fellow-citizens, while they were exempted from every duty which was incompatible with their religion. This was a boon indeed, and solely due to the especial merit of one individual! Among the various benefits conferred on the Jewish nation by this holy Rabbi, must be numbered the composition of the Misna (written in the year 141) a work of untold merit and usefulness. And now, before passing over a period of 328 years, wherein little else is to be noted than cruelty and persecution to the Jews in whatsoever land they were located, it should be observed that they ever adhered faithfully to their religion. Just 363 years after the Misna was written, the Talmud—that work of past ages and of sages—was completed, and glancing onwards, we find that in the year

590, a kindly spirit toward the Jews began to permeate through Christian countries, for they were permitted to re-open their colleges and received especial favour both at the hand of King Honidus III. and of Pope Gregory the Great. However, at the opening of the Mahometan Æra (622) gloom again overshadowed the prospects of the Jews, who were persecuted, and in some instances put to the sword, on account of their refusal to abandon the faith of their forefathers and adopt the new religion.

Nevertheless, a nation so stedfast to that covenant which had already endured for thousands of years, were not to be thus crushed and exterminated. At once heroes and martyrs, they resolutely resisted all compulsion, doubtless bearing in mind the memorable words of Joshua—ch. 23, v. vi., "Be ye very courageous to keep and to do all that is written in the Book of the Law of Moses; that ye turn not aside therefrom to the right hand or to the left."

For nearly a century after this period the Jews, then dispersed over Europe, were rarely permitted to have a permanent abode, for at the mere instigation of any foe, fanatic, or calumniator, they were invariably expelled from their homesteads after being mulcted of the greater portion of their hard-earned wealth. During these dark ages religion was almost disregarded, and the Holy Volume might have been lost to mankind but for the Jews, who treasured it and never failed to read it in their Synagogues. To their consistency and fortitude, to their firm determination to sacrifice everything rather than their belief, and to their love of the sacred heritage which God had entrusted to their safe keeping, was greatly due the preservation of the Bible and that moral light, which, again breaking on the world, shone brighter and brighter with little intermission in succeeding centuries.

But in the year 714 the Jews again found settled homes, for the Moors, on conquering Spain, not only permitted them to reside within its borders, but even protected and favoured them. Two hundred and thirty-four years, however, elapsed before a Jewish college was founded (948), but shortly after its establishment at Cordova, a galaxy of talent was to be found within its walls, a circumstance which was partially due to the closing of the Babylonian

College, when very many of its members, renowned for their profound erudition, emigrated to Spain, and there issued to the world many works of undoubted value in every branch of learning. Their ranks were further swelled some few years later by the arrival of many learned Rabbis from Persia, where the followers of Moses were again undergoing cruel persecutions. During the next century and a half the Jews lived as peaceful citizens in the Iberian Peninsula. They took no part in the unceasing struggle for power between the Christian Monarchs and the Saracen Chieftains, but by their learning and industry did such good service to the country as to gain the esteem and favour of both Christians and Mahometans. Very many Israelites of distinguished talent flourished at this period, and took rank as eminent statesmen, philosophers, theologians, astronomers, mathematicians, physicians, poets, and linguists. Among the most eminent of these may be mentioned SOLOMON BEN GABRIOL, SAMUEL A. LEVI, ISAAC BEN MOSES, and more especially the two—MOSES ABEN EZRA, whose sublime poetic compositions have been transmitted to us as an heirloom, and form a part of the ritual of the Synagogue at the present day; and SAMUEL IBEN NAGRELA, who was Minister of State for thirty years, and gave entire satisfaction to the several ruling monarchs. He was considered the first Mezzofante, being master of ten languages; he was also a voluminous writer. His nobleness of character, his disinterestedness, his freedom from all arrogance or haughtiness in his high station, his devotion to his people, as well as to their moral and intellectual welfare, and yet more, his true piety made him beloved and respected by all, and at his death he was mourned by the whole population of Granada. Truly, this was a golden era in the history of the Spanish Jews, and indeed in most parts of Europe. This much-enduring people then lived peacefully and unmolested, while they remained ever faithful to the observances and inculcations of their religion.

A change, however, occurred about the year 1096, which seriously affected almost the entire Hebrew nation, and was heralded by the outbreak of the Crusades, otherwise termed the Holy War! This began by the massacre of the Israelites over most parts of Europe, but it was especially in Germany that the most horrible carnage ensued. The barbarity of the infuriated fanatics was then appalling, it knew no bounds; and although many bishops exerted themselves in the cause of humanity, there was little cessation to the fearful sufferings and misery of the Jews; however, like true martyrs and heroes, they yielded up their lives as a voluntary sacrifice at the shrine of their religious belief, and were inhumanly butchered by thousands.

On the commencement of the second Holy War some fifty years later (1146), this unfortunate people again had almost everywhere to encounter the fury of the general populace, and but for the noted St. Bernard, who befriended them, their fate would have been no less sad than before; indeed, from the beginning of the Crusades, just ten years after the time that Saladin took Jerusalem (1187), their position throughout most European countries, but especially in England and France, was most critical; frequently fined, plundered, and tortured without provocation, they seemed to be at the mercy of every foe, whilst every man's hand was upraised against them.

Now, notwithstanding this persecution, they rose higher in various branches of science and learning at this sad and gloomy period of their history than during several preceding centuries. Very many eminent Jews, the ornaments of their age, then flourished, whose works shed an imperishable lustre on Hebrew literature. Among these was ABRAHAM BEN EZRA, who excelled as a philosopher, astronomer, physician, poet, and linguist, whilst his writings were both numerous and diversified. But the star that shone brightest in the galaxy of talent was MAIMONIDES, the most eminent philosopher of his age. No obstacles could daunt him in his self-imposed vocation, that of acquiring and imparting deep learning, and when forced to quit Spanish soil, after an ignorant and bigoted populace had burnt no less than forty Synagogues, and murdered large bodies of his co-religionists, he repaired to Cairo, where he opened an academy of philosophy and Hebrew, to which his fame attracted numerous disciples. His marvellous mental powers shortly brought him into notice, and finally he was promoted to the high post of Minister of State. His various works on Theology, Logic, Medicine, Astronomy, and Philosophy have been universally admired, and it is admitted on all hands that he had advanced in knowledge far beyond his time, and had no compeer either in his nation or his age. Milman, in his "History of the Jews," vol. 3, thus writes concerning him:—"The wise Maimonides, the first who, instead of gazing with blind adoration and unintelligent wonder at the great fabric of the Mosaic law, dared to survey it with the searching eye of reason, and was rewarded by discovering the indelible marks of the Divine wisdom and goodness." Not only did he remain steadfast to his religion, but he also exhorted his brethren in faith to adhere strictly to their belief, and all his works clearly show forth the beauty, the sublimity of the Mosaic dispensation. While renowned for a learning that has rarely or never been surpassed, and a liberality of views most rare in those days, his meed of praise assuredly does not rest there, for besides being a man of comprehensive erudition, he proved himself to be possessed of deep, earnest, religious feelings, as testified by his unblemished life; ambition never swayed his mind, while the passions of anger and revenge were alike strangers to him. He observed every ordinance of his faith with the utmost rigour, visited the tomb of the Patriarchs at Hebron, frequently fasted, devoting the day to prayer, and ever sought to relieve the poor and distressed. To this excellent and pious man the Jews owe the composition of the thirteen "Articles of Faith," which must ever form a portion of the ritual of the Synagogue. His "Commentary on the Mishna" was acknowledged by his contemporaries, as well as by posterity to be a master-piece of the utmost importance, and again, his "Mishna Torah," a book in which he compiled the entire Talmudic laws and simplified them, was equally useful and worthy of his high repute. His death, which took place in the year 1204, was considered a national misfortune by the Egyptians, as well as by the Jews; they observed a general mourning for three days and called it the lamentable year, whilst a fast was observed at Jerusalem. Here, indeed, was one of the shining lights in Israel, a light which the surrounding darkness was powerless to dim or obscure, and as the truly virtuous and devout Jew, Maimonides has thrown a glorious halo over the entire Jewish nation.

It was about the year 1200 that the condition of the Jews was again ameliorated in many countries of Europe. The great and good King Phillip Augustus, towards the close of his reign, invited them to return to France, and gave them many privileges; Pope Innocent III., one of the most enlightened men that had ever existed, also befriended them; even the rapacious King John of England granted them a charter, wherein they were exempted from many past restrictions and allowed certain covetted advantages, among which was the power of the Rabbis to decide differences in accordance with the Jewish law; all of which privileges were, however, paid for, though faithlessly withheld at times. Frederick II. of Germany also defended them against oppression and ill-treatment, while Alphonso IX. of Spain showed them peculiar favour, exonerating them from the payment of tithes, permitting them to acquire landed property, and protecting them in the free exercise of their religion. But in England this happier state of things only lasted about 30 years, at the expiration of which time the Jews again had to submit to extortion, nor were they spared fresh indignities, their Synagogues being confiscated and turned into churches; indeed, their lot would have been still more deplorable but for Pope Gregory IX., who upheld their cause, and made a formal protest against such acts of spoliation. The year 1236 also proved a memorable epoch in the history of the Spanish Jews. The Caliphs of the Moorish provinces had to surrender Cordova, the capital, to the victorious forces of King Ferdinand, and then, seeing only fresh trials and calamities awaiting them by this change of dynasty, the Jews quitted with regret that city which had become dear to them from the tranquillity they had there enjoyed for centuries under the Moslem rule, and "through the reminiscences of the glory shed by their scholars on the literary character of the Hebrew nation."*

We may well pass over the next 170 years, during which long term the Jews had to submit to every class of extortion and were made to suffer fearfully throughout the European continent. They encountered every conceivable hindrance to the acquirement of wealth and to the cultivation of knowledge, and to this cause must

---

* E. H. Lindo's "History of the Jews of Spain."

be attributed the paucity of distinguished hebraists and linguists who flourished at this period. But though weighed down by systematic oppression and untold barbarities, the chosen people nevertheless remained true to their faith, and numbers perished for its sake. But in the beginning of the 15th century there was a slight improvement in their condition in some of the smaller states of Europe—notably, in the city of Bologna, where a magnificent Synagogue was erected by the Jews, and every protection and encouragement afforded them, whilst at Venice they were even permitted to establish a Bank. Pope Nicholas V. not only protected the Jews in his own dominions, but befriended them at the Courts of Spain and France, where prejudice, intolerance, and fanaticism were still rampant, and showed their venom in deeds of rapacity and violence; while Louis X. of Bavaria (1454) mercilessly ordered the whole of his Jewish subjects, located in no less than forty cities, to quit his territory in one day! Nor was this cruel expulsion—the more cruel because so sudden—confined to that country alone: the example was followed at Trent, in Silesia, and finally in Spain (1492), where the numberless benefits conferred on the country in past centuries by illustrious Jews, through the medium of commerce, navigation, medicine, literature, and science, were altogether forgotten or ignored. The spirit of fanaticism, led by that bloodthirsty and intolerant monster of iniquity, the Inquisitor Torquamada, counteracted all other considerations, and without the slightest provocation on the part of the Jews, on a fixed day no less than one hundred and seventy thousand families, or about eight hundred thousand souls, were forced to quit that soil upon which numerous generations of their ancestors had flourished and been laid to rest, many, very many, to perish miserably at sea, the remainder to undergo innumerable privations and trials before finding a new home in distant lands.

We may here quote an important extract on this subject from the writings of the chief actor in the drama, DON ISAAC ABARBANEL, then finance minister to Ferdinand and Isabella,— " I was at court and wearied myself to phrenzy with entreaties, but, as the deaf adder, the King closed his ear, the Queen persuading him with all her eloquence to pursue and accomplish what he had begun. My peace, my rest, had gone, trouble was now my portion. And the people bewailed their lot with great lamentations, they greatly mourned; terror and distress were upon them, the like of which had not been since the day that Judah had been driven from his land. They exhorted and encouraged each other to be strong for the sake of religion and the law of God, and to defend them against their hateful persecutors. If they leave us with life we will live, and if they deprive us of it, we shall die; but let us not defile our covenant nor estrange our heart; let us go in the name of the Lord our God. And thus went away in one day from all the royal provinces, young and old, little ones and women, among whom, I myself was, and they went wherever they could go." Truly at no period of their history did the Jews show more true devotion to the religion of their forefathers than during this latter half century. Rather than abjure their faith, they even submitted to become victims to the Inquisition, and thousands were burnt alive, while thousands more were tortured and put to the most excruciating agonies until life was extinct, each one breathing in his mortal hour that prayer which solemnly proclaims the Unity of God. And further, as we have said, the survivors in a body quitted the land that had harboured them for centuries, prepared to encounter trials and dangers rather than become apostates to their faith, by which means they might have gained permission to remain. Some few years later, Portugal followed the example of Spain, and after despoiling the Jews in their midst, expelled them, no way heeding how greatly the country had been enriched and benefitted by their persevering industry in the fields of commerce, literature, and science. Now, what but the knowledge of the persistency and fortitude which characterized the Jews of the Iberian peninsula, would enable us to conceive that, even during this season of sore trouble and persecution, literature was not neglected? Indeed, far from this being the case, no less than thirty-six members of this nation were distinguishing themselves in various branches of learning at the very crisis of their banishment, and among them was ISAAC OROBIO, the author of "Israel Defended," who, in one of his many excellent works, gave a most vivid description of the martyrdom he underwent both in prison and before the dread Tribunal presided over by Torquemada.

The next ninety years (1496 to 1586) was a time of tribulation to the Jews, who found no settled home in all the length and breadth of Europe, with the exception of Poland and the Netherlands. Elsewhere the fanaticism of the populace and the greed of the reigning monarch left them no peace or repose. It was enough for any national misfortune to occur, whether in the shape of some contagious disease such as the plague, a blight, or a deficient harvest, to attribute the blame to the Hebrew people, when immediately uprose a host of cruel persecutors, and sad indeed became their plight. Their quarters were burnt, together with the result of all their literary labours, fines were imposed, tortures inflicted, and in many instances they were even banished. It was well for these forced exiles that Holland not only afforded them a hospitable shelter, but offered every facility whereby they could prosecute their several branches of industry unmolested, while the path of distinction was wide open to them —a path they not only walked with honour to themselves, but with profit to the entire community. It is certain that to Jewish enterprise and intelligence, notable alike on the Exchange and in the market-place, was to be attributed in a great measure the high commercial standing and the commanding position Holland took among the leading nations of Europe at that date. Under the benign sway of the States-General, the Israelites were enabled to open Synagogues and perform every ordinance of their religion without bar or hindrance. Much also did they owe to the Reformation, which movement offered them security from the persecution of ignorant friars and bigoted Dominican Monks, who were ever ready to incite the prejudiced mob against them. Their great acquisition of wealth, with its free disburse in luxuries and splendour, incited no envy, nor did the open display of attachment to their ancestral faith cause umbrage in any quarter. They lived in peace and prospered.

It was, however, only in the year 1586 that symptoms of an amelioration of their condition in other parts of Europe became manifest, and this was due in a great measure to the kindly influence which the excellent Pope, Sextus V., exerted on their behalf. He revoked all decrees against the Jews, admitted them into every part of the Ecclesiastical States, and granted them many privileges, and even monopolies. Civilization, with its natural fruits, humanity and justice, had been making rapid strides during this half century, and none profitted by the happy change more than the hitherto down-trodden, persecuted, and ill-used Israelite. France and Germany soon after saw these sons of toil again within their borders, whilst in 1655 they were permitted to enter England, chiefly through the influence of the great and distinguished Rabbi MANASSAH BEN ISRAEL, who pleaded with Cromwell on behalf of his co-religionists. But the lot of the Jew in all these countries was far from being enviable during the ensuing hundred years; they lived in constant fear, often but too well grounded, frequently had to submit to taunts and indignities, and how strenuously soever they might labour with hand or brain for the public good, they dared not even hope, much less expect, any return in the shape of preferment or distinction. Further, they were constantly subjected to extortion, and heavily mulcted by the several Sovereigns, who, to meet the exigencies of repeated wars of aggression, made them the victims of their greed for dominion and power.

Having now brought our review up to the year 1750, it may be well to see how far the character of the scattered Hebrews had been affected by the ordeals of the past centuries, as well as by the scarcely less endurable species of toleration which had been doled out to them. It is not to be denied that the rancour, the contumely, the scorn, which had so long been heaped upon them, did cause a slight deterioration in their character, and partially sapped some of the better qualities which had distinguished them in happier days. But when it is considered that they were by compulsion penned up in the most squalid quarters, that they were deprived of the privilege of following many an honest and honourable vocation, while compelled to devote their whole energies to the acquirement of money, since through its agency alone could they hope to secure partial freedom from oppression and violence, assuredly those faults or blemishes, which have been unfairly set down by the prejudiced as characteristic traits, are clearly attributable to those who, in a spirit of intolerance, spurned and ill-treated them; indeed, the wonder is that the Jews should have retained so many good qualities under such adverse conditions, except for the fact of their ever strict adherence to their faith, and a ready desire to follow implicitly the moral and sacred obligations inculcated in the Mosaic Code. Clinging to their religion with a tenacity to which History offers no parallel, they learnt through its sublime teachings to bear in a meek and humble spirit that which most galls and depresses the mind of man, viz., ridicule, calumny, hatred, and injustice. This, at least, is certain, that the descendants of those who in times of the direst persecution clung tenaciously to their faith even at the expense of life itself, never wavered, though contempt and ignominy were the sole rewards they reaped for a strict adherence to that religion in which they conscientiously believed, but silently, patiently, they "fought the good fight," and finally gained a glorious victory—a victory over time, events, and prejudice; a victory that ensured to their offspring a goodly heritage, a precious heirloom.

Now, although it must be acknowledged that

the bulk of the Jewish people had lost under sinister influences and discouragements, some of that "juste fierté" which marked the character of their ancestors, it yet needs little demonstration to prove that enough elasticity was left for them to rise as soon as the intolerable weights which had dragged them down were removed; and for this purpose it will suffice to cast a glance on some few important events concerning the Jews that occurred after the middle of the 18th century, which indeed proved the turning point in their history. Who can doubt that as good and useful citizens they had lived down prejudice, when we find that not only were equal privileges with their fellow-countrymen conferred on them by Joseph II. of Germany, (1780), by Louis XVI. of France (1791), by William IV. of England (1831), by the Sovereign of Denmark in 1814, of Austria in 1815, and Portugal in 1820, but that preferment was not slow to follow in every country, excepting indeed, Russia, whence they were expelled by Peter the Great? Wisely profitting by the fair field which had thus been opened to them, many Jews rose high in every branch of industry and in every walk of life, while not a few reaped honours and dignities. Now while civilization, together with a more advanced standard of popular education, had been partly instrumental in bringing about this happy change, it was likewise in no small measure due to the high moral character and the great abilities of many individual Jews, who, indefatigable in cultivating their richly gifted minds, and ever sedulous in their various pursuits or vocations, helped to throw a lustre on their age, and thereby gained for themselves, as also for their co-religionists, the respect and goodwill of the enlightened of all nations.

Foremost among those who adorned the world at that period of its history, and gave an impetus to the more kindly feeling towards the Jews, which was gradually usurping the place of prejudice and intolerance, must undoubtedly be reckoned *Moses Mendelssohn*, and we will conclude this chapter with a brief summary of the life of this distinguished scholar, philosopher, and truly pious Israelite. Born of humble parents, he was early forced to quit home, and for years found no settled resting place, or employment which could bring him means of subsistence, thence often was he dependent on the charity of his co-religionists. Nevertheless, under ever-recurring difficulties and discouragements, he found time to cultivate a highly gifted intellect, and by unceasing mental labour, became one of the great philosophers of his age. It has been generally acknowledged that the German language was in part indebted to him for its development. He certainly was one of the most profound and patient thinkers of that era, whilst, at the same time, he was noted for modesty, amiability, and true piety. That so good, so religious a Jew should withstand every effort which the great Lavater, with ill-judged zeal, made for his conversion, was a matter of course; nevertheless, the repeated attacks upon his belief, his conviction, greatly distressed him, so much so, indeed, as finally to undermine his health, which he never fully recovered, though he sought repose and temporarily desisted from his mental labours. A few extracts from his letters to Deacon Lavater will best serve to illustrate the tenor of his life, since they will show the calibre of his mind, also proving his utter hopelessness, as a Jew, to gain preferment, besides testifying that he not only earnestly studied his religion, but when once fully satisfied of its truth, he steadfastly adhered to his faith till finally summoned to his eternal home. He thus wrote, " My scruples against entering into religious controversy have been neither weakness nor timidity. I can say that it was not yesterday I began to examine my religion ; for I very early felt the duty of trying my opinions and my actions, and if I have devoted my leisure hours to science and polite literature, it has been almost solely as a preparation to this necessary trial, other motives I could not have had. In my situation, I could not expect the least temporal advantages from the sciences. I knew too well that I could not find prosperity in the world by such means. And pleasure, oh ! my esteemed philanthropist ! the condition to which my brethren in faith are condemned in civil life is so far removed from all free exercises of the powers of the mind, that I certainly could not increase my contentment by learning to know the rights of humanity on their true side. I avoid a nearer explanation on this point. He who knows our condition, and has a humane heart, will feel more than I can express. After the inquiry of many years, if the "decision had not been perfectly in favour of my religion it would have been necessarily known by a public act. I cannot imagine what should bind me to a religion in appearance so severe and so generally despised, if I were not in my heart persuaded of its truth. . . . And I here testify in the name of the God of truth, your and my Creator and Father, by whom you have in your dedication conjured me, that I will retain my principles so long as my soul retains its nature. My remoteness from your religion, which I avowed to you, has, in the meanwhile, in no respect diminished. . . . There are certain inquiries which one must at some time of one's life have ended, in order to proceed further. I may assert that, with respect to religion, I have done this several years ago. I have read, compared, reflected, and held fast to that which I thought good. . . . My religion, my philosophy, my situation in civil life, all give me the strongest motives to avoid all religious disputes, and in public writings to speak only of those truths which are equally important to all religions. . . . I wish to be able to destroy the contemptuous opinion which is generally formed of a Jew; not by "controversial writings, but by virtue. . . . Various are the motives which my religion and my philosophy furnish, and induce me carefully to avoid religious disputes, added to the domestic situation in which I live amongst my fellow-men. I am a member of an oppressed people, who must implore shelter and protection from the ruling nation, and even this it obtains not everywhere, and nowhere without limitations. My brethren in faith are willing to renounce liberties which are granted to all other classes of men, and are contented if they are tolerated and protected. They esteem it no small act of beneficence in the nation which receives them only on tolerable conditions, since, in many states, even residence is refused them. . . . But the solemn appeal of a Lavater compels me, at last, openly to declare my mode of thinking, that no one may interpret a silence too long preserved, into confession or contempt." And truly the acts of Mendelssohn corresponded with his words, for he sedulously sought to promote the instruction and well-being of his people; he showed himself deeply anxious that the rising generation should gain the esteem of the Christian population, and thus be admitted into society; in a word, he laboured to do the largest amount of good he could, and met his reward in so far that he secured many valued friends (Lessing foremost among them) and at his death in the 57th year of his age (1786) was followed to the grave by many eminent statesmen and scholars, as well as by a large body of his co-religionists. To this day the Jewish nation honour the name of Mendelssohn, and regard the memory of this truly learned, worthy, and pious Jew with feelings of love, admiration, and gratitude.

Having thus brought to a close this short biographical sketch of one of the brightest luminaries in Israel, it may be well, in conclusion, to remark, that reference to the last hundred years of Jewish history is as unnecessary as unadvisable, since the fair and impartial views entertained by many enlightened and unprejudiced Christians in regard to the character of our nation will be found *in extenso* in the third portion of the next chapter.

Without a blot on our escutcheon, and with so many gratifying testimonies to Jewish worth from such high sources, the Jew of the present day has indeed little to fear, but much, very much to hope, if only he remains as in the past, true to himself, true to his religion, true and faithful to his God.

Chapter VI.

It may be as serviceable as interesting now to take a review of the opinions of some of the most enlightened and learned Christians on three of the subjects under consideration:—1stly, The Unity of God; 2ndly, The beauty and usefulness of the Mosaic laws; and 3rdly, The Jewish characteristics, moral, intellectual and physical; again, those extracts may with advantage be supplemented by others taken from works penned by Jews of acknowledged literary eminence, and noted for their historical research. Among those Christian writers who have treated on the Unity of God, we may mention the name of

JOHN LOCKE, who thus wrote:—"*Non Trinitas*—Because it subverteth the Unity of God, introducing three Gods. Because it is inconsistent with the rule of prayer; for, if God be three persons, how can we pray to Him through His Son for His Spirit?" And again, "There be a multitude "of texts that deny those things of Christ which cannot be denied of God, and that affirm such things of him that cannot agree to him if he were a person of God." And in his Essay on the Human Understanding, we read, "Among all the ideas that we have, as there is none suggested to the mind by more ways, so there is none more simple than that of Unity or One. It has no shadow of variety or composition in it; every object our senses are employed about, every idea in our understandings, every thought in our minds, brings this idea along with it, and, therefore, it is the most intimate to our thoughts, as well as it is in its agreement to all other things, the most universal idea we have." Again, "Every deity that the heathen world owned above one, was an infallible evidence of their ignorance of Him, and a proof that they had no true notion of God, where unity, infinity, and eternity were excluded."

MILTON has thus written, "It is evident from numberless passages of Scripture, that there is but one true, independent, and supreme God; one such as the Jews, the people of God, have always considered Him." Again, "Since Christ not only bears the name of the only begotten

"Son of God, but is also several times called in the Scriptures, God, notwithstanding the universal doctrine that there is but one God, it appeared to many that there was an inconsistency in this, which gave rise to an hypothesis, no less strange than repugnant to reason, that the Son, although personally and numerically another, was yet essentially one with the Father, and that thus the Unity of God was preserved. But unless the terms Unity and Duality be not signs of the same ideas to God which they present us, it would have been to no purpose that God had so repeatedly inculcated the First Commandment, that He was the one and only God, if another could be said to exist besides, who also himself ought to be believed in as the one God. . . . Unity and Duality cannot consist of the one and the same substance. God is one ens, not two, one essence, and if two persons be assigned to one essence, it involves a contradiction of terms, by representing the essence as at once simple and compound. If one divine essence be common to two persons, that essence or divinity will either be in a relation of a whole to its parts or of a genus to its several species. . . Nothing can be more clear

"than that it was the opinion of the Scribes as well as of the other Jews, that by the Unity of God is intended the oneness of His person."
. . . . "It was fitting and highly agreeable to reason, that what was the first, and consequently the greatest, Commandment, scrupulous obedience to which was required by God, should be delivered in so plain a manner, that nothing ambiguous or obscure in its terms could lead His worshippers into error, or keep them in suspense or doubt. And thus the Israelites, under the Law and the Prophets, always understood it to mean that God was numerically one God, that besides Him there was no other, much less an equal. For those disputants of the school had not yet appeared, who, depending on their own sagacity, or rather on arguments of a purely contradictory tendency, cast a doubt on that very unity of God which they pretended to assert. But as the Diety can do nothing which involves a contradiction, so also, nothing can be said of the one God which is inconsistent with His unity, and which implies at the same time the unity and plurality of the Godhead. Though all this be so self-evident, it is wonderful with what futile subtleties, or rather, with

"what juggling artifices, certain individuals have endeavoured to obscure or elude the plain meaning of passages proclaiming the Father alone as a self-existent God." And in his "Paradise Regained," Milton makes these words proceed from the mouth of the Deity, "This perfect man, by *merit* called my son;" and again, when addressing God, he says, "Him *second to Thee*, offered to die, &c."

Sir Isaac Newton also thus refers to the Unity of God, " In all that vehement, universal, and lasting controversy about the Trinity in Jerome's time, and both before and long enough after it, this text of "the Three in Heaven," was never once thought of. It is now in every body's mouth and accounted the main text for the business, and would assuredly have been so too with them, had it been in their books." Again, "Even Cyprian's own words do plainly make for the interpretation (three distinct Beings) as it is in the baptism; the place from which they (the Christians) *tried* at first to derive the Trinity." And again, in alluding to I. Tim. ch. 3, v. xvi., 'God was manifest in the flesh,' he says, "In all the times of the hot and lasting Arian controversy it never came "into play, though now that those disputes are over, it is thought one of the most pertinent texts for the business." As has been observed, "Newton could hardly have written thus had he not regarded these doctrines as gross corruptions of the primitive Christian Faith."

From the *Christian Examiner:*—"We can now bring forward the three greatest and noblest minds of modern times, and we may add of the Christian era, as witnesses to the great truth of the Divine Unity, and with Milton, Locke, and Newton, in our front, we want no others to oppose to a whole array of great names on the opposite side. They came to this subject in the fullness of their strength, with free minds open to truth, and with unstained purity of life. They came to it in an age when the doctrine of the Trinity was instilled by education and upheld by the authority of the Church and by *penal laws.*° And what did these great and

---

° In the *Toleration Act* passed in 1688, before Newton had sent his dissertation to Locke, an exception was made of those who wrote against the doctrine of the Trinity (I. William and Mary, ch. xviii., s. 17). In the act for the suppression of blasphemy and profaneness, it was provided that whoever, by printing or advisably speaking, denied any one of the persons of the Holy Trinity to be God, should, for the first offence be disabled to have any office or emolument, or any profits appertaining thereunto.

"good men discover in the Scriptures? A triple divinity? three infinite objects of worship, three persons, each of whom possesses his own distinct offices, yet shares in the Godhead with the rest? No! Scripture taught them to bow reverently before the One Infinite Father, and to ascribe to Him alone, supreme, self-existent divinity."

CHANNING in a discourse on this subject, says, "We believe in the doctrine of God's *Unity*, or that there is one God, and one only. To this truth we give infinite importance, and it seems to us exceedingly plain. We object to the doctrine of the Trinity, that whilst acknowledging in words, it subverts in effect, the unity of God. According to this doctrine there are three infinite and equal persons, possessing supreme divinity, called the Father, Son, and Holy Ghost. They performed different parts in man's redemption, each having his appropriate office, and neither doing the work of the other. The Son is Mediator and not the Father. The Father sends the Son, and is not Himself sent; nor is He conscious, like the Son, of taking flesh. Here, then, we have three intelligent agents, possessed of "different consciousness, different wills, performing different acts, and sustaining different relations, and if these things do not imply and constitute three minds or beings, we are utterly at a loss to know how three minds or beings are to be formed. We are astonished that any man can read the New Testament and avoid the conviction that the Father alone is God, and we protest against the irrational and unscriptural doctrine of the Trinity. Were it true, it must, from its difficulty, singularity and importance, have been laid down with great clearness and stated with all possible precision. But where does this statement appear? We ask for one, one only, passage, in which we are told that He is a threefold being, or that He is three persons; on the contrary, in the New Testament He is always spoken of in the singular number. We have further objections to this doctrine, drawn from its practical influence. We regard it as unfavourable to devotion, by dividing and distracting the mind in its communion with God. It is a great excellence of the doctrine of God's unity, that it offers to us *one object* of supreme homage, adoration and love. . . . True piety, when "directed to an undivided Deity, has a chasteness, a singleness, most favourable to religious awe and love. . . . But the doctrine of the Trinity injures devotion, by taking from the Father the supreme affection, which is His due, and transferring it to the Son. This is a most important view. That Jesus Christ, if exalted into the infinite Divinity, should be more interesting than the Father, is precisely what might be expected from the principles of human nature. Men want an object of worship like themselves, and the great secret of idolatry lies in this propensity. . . . A God clothed in our form, and feeling our wants and sorrows, speaks to our weak nature more strongly than a Father in heaven, a pure spirit, invisible and unapproachable, save by the reflecting and purified mind. Again, we complain of the doctrine of the Trinity, that, not satisfied with making God three beings, it makes Jesus Christ two beings, and thus introduces infinite confusion into our conceptions of his character. . . . The doctrine that one and the same person should have two consciousnesses, two wills, two souls, infinitely different from each other, this we think an enormous tax on human "credulity, and if a doctrine so strange, so difficult, so remote from all the previous conceptions of men, be indeed a part and an essential part of revelation, it must be taught with great distinctness, yet we do not find any plain, direct passage where Christ is said to be composed of two minds, yet constituting one person. . . . Thus, for the purpose of reconciling certain difficult passages ascribing to Jesus Christ human and other divine properties, we must invent an hypothesis vastly more difficult, and involving gross absurdity. We are to find our way out of a labyrinth by a clue which conducts us into mazes infinitely more inextricable. And again, in the Scriptures our Heavenly Father is always represented as the sole original spring and first cause of our salvation, and let no one presume to divide His glory with another." Many other passages to like effect might be selected from the writings of this eminent Unitarian, but here is surely ample to show that enlightened men of the Christian faith do not run counter to the grand, the fundamental principle of Judaism.

We proceed next to give in a few words the views of another and yet higher authority in Divinity.

Dr. Priestly wrote: "The Hebrew Scriptures declare that God is one, and that there is no God besides Him. This was a truth well known to the Jews from the earliest times. Jesus taught nothing new when he upheld this great doctrine. The answer made by the Jewish scribe, 'Master, thou hast said the truth, for there is One God, and there is none other but He,' shows that Jesus and his hearers were agreed on this point." Again, "The most essential articles of pure Christianity I consider to be the proper *unity of God* and the proper *humanity of Christ*. The Unity of God is a doctrine on which the greatest stress is laid in the whole system of revelation. To guard this most important article was the principal object of the Jewish religion. And again, Paul giving what may be called the Christian Creed, says, Tim. ch. 2, *v.* v., 'There is one God and one Mediator between God and men, the man Christ Jesus.' He does not say, 'the God, the God-man,' but simply '*the man* Jesus,' and nothing can be alleged from the New Testament in favour of any higher nature of Christ, except a few passages interpreted without any regard to the context."

The Rev. J. W. Fox, in a Lecture on this subject, says, "The doctrine of the Divine Unity is the centre of religious truth, the source of light and goodness in the heart. There can be but one God, but one omnipotent, infinite, uncaused Being. This truth is the religion of the Bible. Unitarians are not and have not been of one opinion about any but this fundamental doctrine. This one doctrine they find taught through the whole of Scripture. Judaism is unitarian; its teachings in the Old Testament are strongly unitarian. The New Testament teaches it by direct assertions, as well as by the absence of all contradictions of it. The Mahommetans are strictly Unitarians. In India and China there have been philosophers who taught a pure worship of one God. The wisest and best philosophers of Greece and Rome rose above the superstitions of their age, and taught that there was really but one God."

SELTON on Hindüs Worship: "All that has been handed down by oral tradition seems to confirm the hypothesis that the Hindüs were worshippers of one God only, whom they designated 'the Breathing Soul,' a Spiritual Supreme Being, coeval with the formation of the world, everlasting, permeating all space, the beneficent disposer of events."

Rev. G. Vance Smith: "There are three passages in the New Testament in reference to the Trinity, one of them, however, being the worthless interpolated verse in the First Epistle of John. Thus there are left two passages which are usually supposed, clearly and unquestionably to express the doctrine of three Divine persons; two only, be it remembered, out of the whole extent of the Bible. ... Throughout the Biblical writings, where is there any trace of a radical change in the mode of conceiving of the Oneness of God? Where do we find some positive declaration, plainly announcing the new doctrine? When and where precisely in the teachings of Scripture is the new idea of a Divine plurality, a Divine threeness, first distinctly introduced as the correction or completion of the older doctrine? Where is the ancient idea of One Jehovah besides whom there is no other God, modified and changed into a trinity of persons, each of whom is God as much as either of the others? Can any one say:—'Here the doctrine of the threefold nature of the Godhead was first revealed?' &c."

EARL RUSSELL, in his "Essays on the History of the Christian Religion," writes thus: "The first thing we should wish to learn is the character assumed by Christ Himself, and we cannot but be struck with the consistency of this declaration, whether made to the Jews or to his faithful and intimate disciples—the unity of God, declared by Moses, "I am the Lord thy God, thou shalt have none other gods but Me," a doctrine embraced by Socrates, by Plato, by Cicero, and by the most enlightened of the Pagans."

The Rev. H. HARRIS remarked on this doctrine: "Not once in the pages of the Bible is the word Trinity to be found, and the only passage which speaks of three persons making one is undoubtedly spurious. After many years of doubt and hesitation, the good Dr. WATTS became convinced of the error of his early faith and took up in its stead the doctrine of the unity of God." And again: "For the first 150 years the opinions of the Christians were strictly unitarian. From that time till the Council of Nicea in 325, various corruptions were added to Christianity. . . . If these then be facts, let us be among those who hold fast to what Sir Isaac Newton justly called the 'long lost truth' of the Unity of God."

The Trinity, so called, was never acknowledged in any manner whatever by our Society (*The Quakers*), the very term even is disallowed by our body, as being nowhere to be found in the Holy Scriptures. — *Monthly Repository*, vol. 8.

MARTIN LUTHER thus wrote (Postil Major, fol. 282): "The word Trinity sounds oddly and is a human invention. It were better to call Almighty God, God, than Trinity."

Finally JOHN CALVIN (Tract Theol. pp. 796) says: "I like not the prayer, O, holy, blessed glorious Trinity. It savours of barbarity. The word Trinity is barbarous, insipid, profane, a human invention, grounded on no testimony of God's word."

With these two particularly strong and all important protests against the Trinity we conclude this subject, although it would be easy to add very many more extracts to like effect, embracing the forcible argument that *only two verses* in the New Testament express the doctrine of three Divine persons, viz.: Mat. ch. 28, *v.* xix, and 2 Cor. ch. 13, *v.* iv, while not only the Old Testament abounds in passages emphatically declaring the Unity of God, but even in the

Gospel itself are to be found numerous texts inculcating that doctrine, and perhaps none more clearly, more explicitly, than that in Mark ch. 17, *v.* xxix.: "And Jesus answered (the Scribe) thus: 'The first of all the Commandments is, Hear, O Israel, the Lord *our* God is one Lord.'"

We will now proceed to our second subject, and give brief extracts from the writings of several eminent Christians on the beauty and usefulness of the Mosaic laws.

PRIESTLY thus alludes to them: "There are, it is acknowledged, several articles in the institutions of Moses for which we are not able to assign satisfactory reasons, but this cannot be thought extraordinary, considering that their antiquity is so great, and that they were adapted to a state of manners, opinions, and other circumstances of those remote times with which we are but imperfectly acquainted. Neither are we able fully to satisfy ourselves with respect to many particulars in the system of nature, which, notwithstanding, we have no doubt came from God. And the more attention we give to both, the more reason do we discover for those circumstances which at first appeared the most objec-

"tionable. *The better we understand them both, the more reason do we see to admire them*, and to be satisfied that they were ordained by a wisdom more than human." Again: "The great object of the Hebrew religion was to preserve in the world, the important knowledge of the Unity of God and of His administration of the affairs of the world in opposition to the universally prevailing polytheism and idolatry." . . "The ultimate aim of this extraordinary dispensation was by no means the honour or advantage of one particular nation, *but by their history and discipline the great universal Parent gives the most important lessons to all His offspring of mankind.* By means of this one nation, have all other nations that have acquired the knowledge, been taught the great doctrine of the Unity of God, and the purity of His worship. In no case has the mere reason of man been sufficient for this salutary purpose. By this means the Supreme Being has preserved upon the minds of men a sense of their dependence on Himself and of their obligation to Him . . . . of their common relation to one God and Father, and *thereby to consider each other as brethren* entitled to every kind office that they can render to each other."

Professor Newman says: "From the Jews the Christians derive nearly all that is valuable in their religion."

Isaac D'Israeli thus wrote: "The law of Moses can never fall into neglect while the principle of Judaism acts on its people, for it possesses a self-regenerating power. The Law is not locked up in a clasped volume, to be consulted only by the administrators of the Law, but it is thrown open among the people. It is one of the thoughts of Pascal, to show the distinction between a false and a true revelation, that Mahomet, in order that his own code might subsist, prohibited its reading, but Moses, that his own should subsist, ordered that all the world should read it."

Leland, in his work, "Divine Authority of the Old and New Testament," thus sums up, "At the time when the Law was given, idolatry had made very great progress, things were growing worse and worse, and it is highly probable that, if God had not extraordinarily interposed, true religion would have been lost among men. It pleased Him, therefore, in this state of things, to select a nation to Himself, among whom the knowledge and the worship of the "true God should be preserved. And to that end He first exerted his own Almighty power and goodness in delivering that nation from a state of slavery, *and then caused the most pure and excellent laws* to be given unto them, which were promulgated with the greatest solemnity, and attested by the most amazing and unparalleled miracles. And in order the more effectively to answer the main design He had in view, it pleased Him to enter into a peculiar relation to that people, and to take them for His own, by a solemn public act or covenant. . . . And if we enquire into the nature of the Laws that were given them, the main design seems evidently to be this, to preserve them from idolatry and wickedness, and to engage them in the worship of the only true God and the practice of righteousness. They are therein strictly commanded to worship and serve the Lord God and Him alone, the Eternal and self-existant Jehovah ; to love Him with all their hearts and souls, to fear Him and to dread His displeasure above all things, to put their whole trust and confidence in Him, to submit themselves cheerfully to His rightful authority, and to obey all His commands. And as the

"Law of Moses directs and instructs them in the duties they more immediately owe to God, so also in those they owe to one another. It forbids in the strongest manner all malice, wrath, and bitterness; all injustice, fraud, violence, and oppression; all fornication, adultery, and uncleanness; all falsehood, guile, deceit, and even all covetousness; *it not only requires exact truth and fidelity, a strict inviolable honesty in our dealings towards all men, but it expressly requires us to love our neighbours as ourselves;* to be ready to do good to one another on all occasions, yea, even to our enemies themselves; to show mercy to the poor, the indigent and destitute, strangers, and servants. *These moral precepts are such, as if duly practised and obeyed, could not fail to make that nation happy.* Moses might, therefore, justly represent these laws and statutes as sufficient to make them 'a wise and understanding people,' and exclaim, 'What nation is there so great, that hath statutes and judgments so righteous, as the law which I set before you this day?'"

Quoting again from PRIESTLEY'S Institutes, "An habitual regard to God and a peaceful "trust in Him is taught in the Bible as the best support under the difficulties of life; we meet there with feelings of hope and joy in trial, such as the heathens, from the want of an enlightened faith in God to rest them on, could have no idea of. Thus the Hebrew religion builds its moral teachings upon a knowledge of God's character. It gives us for our measure of excellence, God's own perfection; it enforces our endeavours to do right by the command of a righteous God who loves righteousness and spurs us forward by placing before us his affection to us, his encouragement of our efforts."

By COLLIN DE PLANCY: "The Jewish religion is a venerable mother, whose age is lost in the obscurity of time. She has given birth to two daughters, the Christian religion and the Mahommetan. They glory in being descended from her,—and desire nothing so much as to see her exterminated. They approve all she has done before being a mother, and condemn all she has done since, although her conduct has been always nearly the same; in a word, they have for her at the same time, admiration and horror."

We meet in the writing of the Rev. H. JOHNSTONE, the following: "I hope that some day human society may be so far improved as to be able to follow the dictates of the Divine-given Jewish Code. It is a sad error to suppose that the Lord, having once thought the Jewish laws good, could think them so no longer. Taking into consideration the difference in the climate or in the ages, I cannot hesitate in believing that wherever our civil laws disagree with those that have received the sanction of God, we *ought to count them as imperfect and open to amendment*. And if our actual social condition impedes all amendment, that condition is a deplorable evil."

PASCAL: "The Jewish religion must assuredly be divine, considering whence it proceeded, its duration, its perpetuity, *its high moral, its practicability*, its doctrines, and its results. Again, the religion of the Jew may seem to draw its strength from its founder, Abraham, its ceremonies, the Temple at Jerusalem, &c.; but I say that *it solely derives its vitality from the love of God !*"

We conclude this portion of our subject with a brief extract from "Lectures in the East," by

DEAN STANLEY: "There is the humanity which ran through the Law of Israel, and which so rarely appears in the ancient Egyptian religion. The sons of Israel were, by the very recollection of their own bondage, entreated to be kind to all those in inferior condition to themselves. In the version of the Ten Commandments in Deuteronomy, this is the reason given for observing the rest of the Sabbath, 'That thy man-servant and thy maid-servant may rest as well as thou.' And again, 'It was reserved for Moses to make the high truth of One Presiding Spirit the inheritance of all classes alike. That *all* should know that there is One and the same God for *all*, . . . and that we may have endless comfort in the thought that we are in the hands of One overruling God, who makes all things work together for the best."

Passing to the 3rd subject; The Christian view in regard to the Jewish people and to their characteristics, moral, intellectual, and physical, we extract the following from a speech delivered by Monsr. de TALLEYRAND:—"There can be no difference between the Jews and ourselves but in the exercise of their religious worship; take "that away, what can we see in them but fellow citizens and brothers? Were it otherwise, it would be religion that gives civil and political rights; but it is birth, domicile or property that confers them. If we reject the Israelites as Jews, we punish them for being born in one religion rather than another; this is a manifest infraction of all laws, human or civil."

BURDER (On Religious Ceremonies): "Doubtless important designs are to be answered by the providence of God in preserving the Jews in so extraordinary a manner. When we meet with one of the sons of Abraham (and in what place are they not to be met with?) we see a miracle —a living confirmation of the Divine veracity— a proof that the Bible is true, and an indubitable testimony that there is a God who judgeth the earth."

Count de MIRABEAU thus wrote: "Why should not the Jews think themselves the greatest of men, when, by a miracle greater than those of their ancient history, they exist still, despite the tyranny and oppression of every nation! Few can, even in favour of great talent and eminent virtues, forgive to a Hebrew the sin of being born a Jew, although it is from their

"Sacred Book that nations have borrowed all their dogmas. . . . Those only who would themselves permit fraud towards a Hebrew, accuse him of daring in virtue of his faith to practise deception towards the followers of other religions, and the bigotted priests who have collected calumnious tales concerning the Jews, have only betrayed their own prejudices."

The Rev. JOHN MILLS thus spoke at a public meeting:—" We owe the Jews a greater debt than that of common humanity. We owe a debt to every nation which has added to the comforts, and aided in the improvement of the human race. Who can reflect, for example, upon the poets, the historians, the philosophers, and artists of ancient Greece without feeling, gladly feeling, that futurity will ever be indebted to them? Well, *how much more to the Jews?* They gave us the Bible, the book of books, which independent of its inspiration, is a more effective instrument to strengthen the intellect as well as to improve the heart, than any other work the world ever saw. This blessed Book was first written and promulgated by the Jews, and we sympathize, deeply sympathize, with the children for the Father's sake."

From the writings of the Rev. THOS. RAFFLES: "We are laid under the deepest obligation to the Jews. There is nothing grand or good that we possess, but we are indebted to that people. The most ancient and most authentic of all historians was a Jew, and what poets, for sublimity and grandeur, can compare with theirs? But these are minor considerations and matters of trivial moment compared with those spiritual blessings for which we are indebted instrumentally to them. . . . We may not forget that for all the light and religion, for all the peace and joy, for all the hopes and anticipations we derive from the Bible, we owe to the Jews."

The Rev. CHAS. VOYSEY has thus written: "I am thankful to have gained an insight into the most venerable and *most simple of all creeds*. My firm belief is the Jews will never lose their nationality in their indelible and inimitable characteristics."

Extracts from Rev. Father IGNATIUS' Discourse: "It might be said the Jewish people were an insignificant nation, but I assert it was a most important one. . . . One of the chief characteristics of a nation's greatness and a people's power, consists in a rightly balanced "legislation. Now, if we compare the legislation of Moses with that of any other race of people, either of modern times or times gone by, we find that it stands out with a strange uniqueness that startles us. *The legislation of Moses, though it has existed for thousands and thousands of years, has never been added to, never been abstracted from, never been tampered with, or changed to suit the continual changes of nations and politics.* The Jewish legislation began and ended in Moses. They might say this unchangeableness was because the people were content to be overridden and kept down. No. *If ever there was a nation which possessed the determination to exist, to be free, it was the Jewish nation.* Remember the battering rams of Titus and Vespasian against the walls of Jerusalem, where millions of Jews were ready to pour out rivers, nay, oceans of blood for liberty, which is the noblest thing, which is the thing God's spirit teaches us to crave for above all else, because it is the divine right of man. . . . No, the Jews could not be accused of being a cowardly and slavish race; we could not so account for the unchanged existence of their legislation for fifteen centuries, which was a mighty monu-

"ment of an Almighty hand, a practical proof of the Omnipotence of the voice which spoke in thunders on Mount Sinai and in lightning on the peaks of Oreb."

Australian Paper: "What a walking encyclopædia and history is the Jew! What a stretch of imagination just to think that one of the unknown throng of swart Israelites, who listened to the song of Miriam on the Red Sea triumph, should be the progenitor of a people who is intimately associated with the nineteenth century civilisation, and has become one of the principal factors of the greatness and prosperity of unborn nations and communities! Their blood is uncontaminated, their race has a spotless escutcheon; there is no bar sinister in his shield, for *no people have ever been so correct in their morals as the Jews,* and so careful not to contract degenerate alliances. No race seems to have possessed such a wonderful power of recuperation. Driven from their own land, persecuted in every age, driven from country to country by Pagan and by Christian hate, they have survived the sword, the gibbet, and the stake, and are perhaps more numerous to-day than ever they were in the world's "history. A faithful and historic people; who can but admire them?"

The Rev. J. M. Wise, of Chicago thus delivers himself in a lecture—"Like lofty mountains crowned with azure tints and celestial rays, Israel's prophets, bards, kings, heroes, sages, and saints, appear to the watching eye of the devout investigator standing upon the watch-tower of human reason. . . . It is with reverence and awe only that we can approach the history of Israel, while it is impossible to do justice to their vast and deep revelation. . . . During the first period, which terminates with the dispersion among the Assyrians and Babylonians, Israel occupied the position of a pupil under the tuition of the Most High. During nearly nine centuries it studied, and studied well, the lessons of religion, ethics, and politics, and obtained in these abstract sciences, that perfection which the Bible represents. It must have exercised some influence on the surrounding nations by its army, wealth, and eloquence, especially during the reigns of David and Solomon. . . . During the second period, which begins with the first dispersion, and terminates with the last, under the Romans, Israel "occupied the position of the teachers among the nations, and understood its vocation and duty, its great and sublime mission. Historians have hitherto failed to point out the influence of the sons of Israel upon the events which then revolutionized the political and religious institutions over the vast territory over which they were dispersed, but beyond a doubt they were powerful agents, mighty engines in the hands of Providence, to effect and carry out those important revolutions which impelled the human family onward to light and right and forward to truth and justice. . . . In the third period of its history, which begins with the final dispersion and is not yet ended, Israel occupied the position of a guardian of truth, a truth which it had studied during the first period of its history and taught during the second—the divine truth in and for which it lived, struggled and died a thousand deaths, was the only treasure it saved from the ruins of the grandeur which was no more; but this, the only treasure which Israel saved was adamantine. . . . The Jew took his Bible everywhere, and without his stiff-neckedness and obstinacy, that is, without his firmness, fortitude, consis-

"tency, and resolution, without his determination to sacrifice everything except his belief, his conviction, and the sacred heritage which God entrusted to his care and safe keeping, it would most certainly have been lost to the world, and the dark ages must have extended over many a century longer, probably to our very days."

SOUTHEY: "When literature had gone to decay throughout Christendom, the Jews did not partake of the general degradation. They had many professors, whose everlasting lamps were kept trimmed amongst them, and burning clearly, when the light of the Gospel had grown dim in the socket, and monkery and popedom had well nigh extinguished it."

MACAULEY: "There is nothing in the national character of the Jew which unfits him for the highest duties of citizens. In the infancy of civilisation, when our island was as savage as New Guinea, when letters and arts were still unknown to Athens, this condemned people had their splendid Temple, their fleet of merchant ships, their schools of sacred learning, their great statesmen and soldiers, their philosophers, historians and poets. What nation ever contested more manfully against overwhelming "odds for its independence and religion? What nation ever, in its last agonies, gave such signal proofs of what might be accomplished by a brave despair? Let none presume to say there is no genius among the countrymen of Isaiah, no heroism among the descendants of the Maccabees, while it is the Jewish religion which first taught the human race the great lesson of universal charity."

G. C. LEWES (in his "History of Philosophy"): "The part played by the Jews as physicians, merchants, or bankers, has often been appreciated. The part played by them as thinkers has been less frequently mentioned, yet it has been considerable. Ignored by society, the learned Jews gave themselves up to science and to study. Hated and persecuted though they were, their ability and perseverance made them everywhere necessary to princes and to nobles. . . . The learned unsuspectingly submitted their minds to Hebrew thinkers. The facility with which they mastered language made them ready interpreters between Musselmen and Christians. It was through their translators and through their original thinkers that the West became leavened with Greek and Oriental thought."

BASIL MONTAGU: "Of the acuteness of the Jewish intellect it cannot be necessary to adduce proof. It appears in their daily intercourse with us and with each other. Of their affections, who can doubt? The Englishman's fireside is proverbial for domestic happiness, but of all firesides, the Jews', as far as relates to their affections, is the most abundant in good feeling, from the most opulent to the most indigent. Next, as to their orderly conduct as members of society, they are regular and industrious in their habits, cultivating those branches of trade committed to them, and increasing the prosperity of their country by enlarging its commerce. They have ever been loyal subjects and anxious to assist their country, cheerfully pouring out their hoards when the State required it, while one and all, when the occasion arose, enlisted, and would have proved themselves descendants of the noble Maccabees."

Edinburgh Review: "The Jews have been thickly planted in the chief rising seats of civilization and commerce, and in almost every well-known city, we hear of Hebrew settlements more or less considerable in number. Nor is it too much to say, that the influence of "these widely dispersed Jews must have been everywhere felt. *In the case of the Jew alone was religion bound to a law of moral purity.* The Jew only had a conscience in the better and higher sense."

FLEURY: "The people God chose for the purpose of preserving the true religion, form an admirable model, whether it be in their manners, their mode of living, their industry, their urbanity. . . . If we compare the Israelites of old with the Romans, the Greeks, the Egyptians, and the other ancient people most esteemed, our prejudices against them vanish away. We find in them a noble simplicity, and while they had all the good qualities of other nations, they were exempt in a great measure from their defects, for they based their conduct on the true religion which is the foundation of all morality."

Chamber's Cyclopædia : "To enumerate names of those who were and are illustrious in general literature, in law, philosophy, medicine, philology, mathematics, and *belles lettres*, we cannot even attempt, since there is not one country in Europe which does not number Jews among the foremost and most brilliant representatives "of its intellectual progress. Of Germany—considered to be in the vanguard of European learning—the greater part of the professors at its universities are Jews or of Jewish origin: certainly a most startling fact. Another extraordinary fact is that the European press, no less than the European finance, which means the freest developments of all the resources of soil and science for the gigantic enterprises of our day, are to a great extent in their power, while numerous are the names of those who shine in all branches of art, music, sculpture, painting, the drama, &c., all proving how unjust is the reproach of their being an "abstract" people. Briefly—they are, by the unanimous verdict of the historians and the philosophers of our times, reckoned among the chief promoters of the development of humanity and civilization. And what has been their reward? . . . If there be a gradation in suffering, Israel has reached the highest acme; if the long duration of sufferings and the patience with which they are borne, ennobles, the Jews defy the high born of all countries; if a literature is called rich which contains a few classical dramas, what must be said of that tragedy which lasted "a millenium and a half, and was composed and enacted by the heroes themselves?"

JOHN LOCKE: "If Abraham, Isaac, and Jacob, from whom the Jewish nation had their originals, were holy, the branches also that spring from this root are holy, and if those were taken in and engrafted, and have partaken of the blessings promised to Abraham and his seed, be not so conceited of thyself as to show any disrespect to the Jews. If any such vanity possess thee, remember that the privilege which thou hast in being a Christian is derived *to thee* from the promise which was made to Abraham and his seed, but not that accrues to Abraham and his seed *from thee*."

Edinburgh Review: "A singular testimony to the worth of the Jews as citizens, was recorded in the Court of Justice at Nismes, to the effect, that for ten years no one Jew had ever appeared before that Court for either a misdemeanour or a crime, and that as to the accusation of usury, so freely brought against them, only two Jews were prosecuted for this offence in the whole of the South of France, when a thousand Frenchmen had been cited and punished as usurers, and even the criminal "tables here in England show a smaller proportion of Jews brought to justice than of most Christian denominations." And again, "In all countries the Jews have advanced the arts of peace and affronted the national vanities by the success of their undertakings. Their persevering labour, when converted into money, has given them a superiority which has at once roused the envy and the cupidity of the natives, so that their sufferings have been in proportion to their social excellence. It is impossible to say how much the active habits of English trade owe to the example and competition of this people since they have been allowed to settle freely amongst us."

JUDGE MELLOR (1873), summing up a case of offence which, as he said, was calculated to excite the prejudice and violence of the ignorant, thus addressed the Jury—"No man need be ashamed of being a Jew, but under some circumstances (as in the present instance) the name was used as a word of reproach. A Jew had a lineage to be proud of, if anybody had, and the Jews, of all persons in the world, had, in point of race, influenced the destinies of mankind more than any other race. But "independently of Scriptural knowledge, every one should think that there was no impeachment of reproach in the name of Jew."

In the same year, thus spoke at a public meeting the EARL OF SHAFTESBURY: "I have come most gladly to pronounce openly what I have ever felt in secret, that is, my profound veneration and love for the whole mass of the Jewish people. . . . They are the remnants of an ancient nation of great note and fame, who occupied a most distinguished position in the pages of the world's history, and whose glories have never been surpassed. . . They are remarkable for their industry, their truth, and their submission to all the principles of just government, in whatever country they may be placed. They are not behind in any quality that dignifies and adorns men and women in any walk of life, and we should all have a deep interest in the millions of Jewish people who are making their way in every part of the world."

With this high encomium from one of the most distinguished statesmen of the day, we may conclude these extracts—which have been gleaned exclusively from Christian sources—

glad in the thought that so many men of enlightenment, discerning excellent qualities in the Jewish people—qualities which are assuredly the fruits of a strict adherence to their sublime laws—have cast aside all prejudice and generously avowed their recognition of those virtues.

It would be altogether superfluous to enter on the subject of the Unity of God under a Jewish point of view, as it has had our attention in the first chapter of this work, while also the second subject has been treated on at some length in the 4th chapter, thence we proceed at once to give some few extracts from Jewish Authors in regard to the last, and these may be brief, since they could contain little else than a repetition of those facts which have received their due acknowledgment from the many eminent Christians whose remarks and opinions we have quoted in the preceeding pages.

Now the Jews having been frequently accused of lukewarmness in religion at about the time of Jesus Christ, it may be well to hear what the able Historian *Josephus* says on this score, for we may thus be enabled to refute so unjustifiable a charge; we read, "And there came many ten thousands of the Jews to Petronius to offer their petitions to him, that he would not compel them to transgress and violate the law of their forefathers; but if, said they, 'thou art entirely resolved to bring this statue and erect it, *do thou first kill us, for while we are alive, we cannot permit such things as are forbidden us to be done by our Legislator.*' Then on Petronius angrily rejecting their petition, they said, 'Since, therefore, thou art so disposed, O Petronius! that thou wilt not disobey Caius' epistles, *neither will we transgress the commands of our laws*, and as we depend upon the excellency of our laws, and by the labours of our ancestors have continued hitherto without suffering them to be transgressed, we dare not by any means permit ourselves to be so timorous as to transgress those laws out of the fear of death. . . . we should incur the great anger of God, who, even thyself being judge, is superior to Caius.' . . . 'Then Petronius said to them, 'Will you then make war with Cæsar without considering his great preparations for war and your own weakness?' They replied, 'We will not make war with him, *but still we will die before we see our laws transgressed.' So they threw themselves down on their faces and stretched out their throats and said they were ready to be slain, and this they did for forty days together*, and in the meantime left off the tilling of their ground, and that, while the season of the year required them to sow it. Thus they continued firm in their resolution, *and proposed to themselves to die willingly rather than to see the dedication of the statue.*" Lukewarmness to their religion indeed! Where in the annals of history do we read of any people showing such unflinching courage, such determination to resist oppression, such fidelity to their faith and their God? And, again, when Cæsar ordered that a statue should be placed in the Temple they insisted on the observance of their laws and said, 'We offer sacrifice twice every day for Cæsar and for the Roman people, but if he would place the images among them, he must first sacrifice the whole Jewish nation, and that they were ready to expose themselves, together with their children and wives, to be slain. At this Petronius was astonished, and pitied them on account of *the inexpressible sense of religion the men were* under and, that courage of theirs which made them ready to die for it, so they were dismissed."

Hebrew Review (1831): "The Jewish people may fearlessly offer themselves to the strictest scrutiny of their fellow-men, and may feel confident of coming out of it with honour. They have ever shown the qualities of mercy and humanity, and these are the basis on which a large proportion of their virtues are built. They certainly preserve them from the commission of many dreadful crimes and cause them to practice many of those virtues which God has commanded them, and on which the sustaining of the social system so much depends. It is well known that they make the best husbands and wives. Domestic discord is scarcely known among them. Their affection and tenderness towards their offspring is proverbial. Sobriety is so general among them, that it is rare to see a Jew in the shameful state of inebriation. A Jew homicide is so rare that we almost doubt if a single instance can be adduced of one in this country for nearly an entire century, and that it is equally so in all countries where they dwell, we believe we may assert with truth. And be it said, the above remarks apply equally to the humble as to the wealthy class."

On many scores we think it well not to quote any Jewish writer on the subject of the character of the Hebrew people at the present day; this indeed, speaks plainly for itself far more plainly than any words, in their home, in their institutions, in the busy mart, and in the Temple of Worship, but we may, in conclusion, give one extract from a foreign source; it is from *Judge Noah's* address to his Christian countrymen of New York, and speaks volumes for the moral character of our transatlantic brethren. He said: " Dismiss from your hearts all prejudice which still lurks there against our people. They are worthy of your love, your confidence and respect, and that feeling simply arises from your early education. Dismiss it then; be better acquainted with the Jew and learn to estimate his virtues. See him in the bosom of his family, the best of fathers, and the truest of friends. See children, dutiful, affectionate, and devotedly attached, supporting their parents with pride and exultation. See wives the most faithful, mothers the most devoted. Go with me into the haunts of misery, where the daughters of misfortune walk the streets of this great city, and see if among them all you find *one* Jewess. Come with me to the prisons where crime, riots, and vice abounds, and examine whether a Jew is the tenant of a dungeon. Go into your almshouses, and ascertain how many Jews are recipients of your bounty. See them all, the friends of virtue and of temperance, obedient to the laws, and devoted to the country that protects them. Are we not, then, worthy of your confidence and esteem, discharging, as we do, every moral obligation imposed upon us?"

www.ingramcontent.com/pod-product-compliance
Lightning Source LLC
Chambersburg PA
CBHW020247170426
43202CB00008B/258